3+

3/93

Dan —
Pilot's Do Pray —
Just like football —
Coaches — Enjoy —
Doug Rounds

PILOTS ALSO PRAY

PILOTS ALSO PRAY

Lt. TOM HARMON

1944

THOMAS Y. CROWELL COMPANY

NEW YORK

Designed by George Nehrbas

Lithographed in the United States of America

CONTENTS

INTRODUCTION

THIS IS A STORY of a boy whose talent and the use to which he has put it naturally has kept him for most of his life involved in that kind of drama which is stranger than fiction. His family endowed him well. Out of his heritage, rich in fibre, grew a character that from a humble beginning reached the heights of fame and admiration.

It will be an invaluable story many years from now because it is open, honest, free from the need and tendency to color events, conceal their identity, or disguise their purport.

For some time Tom Harmon has been a newspaper celebrity—not an ordinary one—not one of those flaming particles that flare so brightly for a few weeks or months and then vanish completely when their little moment is through. What has happened to Tom Harmon in the following pages is not important but what inspired him is. He had a depth of devotion for his mother and father. His loyalty to family and friends was unexcelled. To be worthy of the trust of others was his greatest ambition. His every effort and act carried with them the burning desire to justify the confidence others placed in him.

His ideals are no different than any other American boy in the service of his country. Like other boys in countless alien fields, he flew over tangled jungles, the hot sands of Africa and the rice paddies of China, ready to pay that last full measure of devotion to a nation that taught us to cherish man's birthright of decency and dignity enough to die for them. If this book even in some small measure offers reassurance to parents of great Americans who have narrowly escaped tragedy or who have lost sons in this terrible conflict, then I am sure it will have achieved success.

His every achievement humbly beseeches parents, sons and all of us to have faith and fidelity in the dark hours of adversity. Tom Harmon was never one to compromise with defeat. He has fought for the right and thereby not infrequently, without his choosing, has created a national sensation. His life has been original and his own description of its elations and disappointments is as unique and interesting as his life itself.

FRITZ CRISLER

THE HARMONS

1

THE WHITE STUCCO HOUSE on the corner seemed to bulge in and out like something in a Disney film with the force of the argument going on inside. At least that is the way the picture has looked in my mind ever since I heard about it some years later.

It was a hot summer day in Rensselaer, Indiana, back in 1919, and the Harmons were at it again. Although I wasn't present as yet, I was the cause of the argument. Sally Harmon, the eldest of the five children, had a definite pain in her seventeen-year-old dignity. Mother Harmon, of all undignified things, was going to produce a sixth little Harmon!

Sally was one of the most popular girls in town, and she felt that she was getting to be quite a young woman of the world. She had a lot of friends, and so far her family had never done anything to embarrass her. But now to think that her own mother was going to have a baby— it was almost more than Sally could stand!

The rest of the family, whose dignity was not quite on Sally's level, thought the idea was great. What was more, they all jumped on Sally for not agreeing with them. Mary Kay, Harold, Louis Jr. and Gene were all agreed that another Harmon would be a fine addition to the world, and although Dad Harmon didn't say very much he was deeply happy about it.

Lou and Rose Harmon were well known to all the folks of the small town, especially to the kids. Mother Harmon was called Aunt Rose by most of the young fry, and it was a rare occasion when her house wasn't swarming with them. It seemed as though kids were her real element, and she was theirs too. It didn't make any difference to her who they were or where they came from, so long as they were friends of the Harmon tribe. They all received a warm welcome in the house of Aunt Rose.

The warm summer months of the year I have in mind went by, and nothing extraordinary happened. Somehow there seemed to be a lighter tone around the house, but otherwise the Harmons went about their business as usual. Now and then there would be arguments or fights, of course, as there are bound to be with five lively Irish children under one roof, and Mother Harmon occasionally had to step into the breach. When she wasn't strong enough to see that justice was dispensed all the way around, Lou Harmon could always be depended upon to come to her assistance. It could never be said that Dad Harmon ever coddled any of his children. They knew from the beginning who wore the pants in the family, and if they ever had any doubts about the matter, they soon found out that their father's ability to throw "pants-warming parties" was as great as ever.

Lou Harmon had been quite a track man in his younger days, and he still kept in fine fighting trim. His boyhood had been spent on a farm in Illinois, and hard work was his element just as kids were his wife's. He never winced at it. "Hard work never hurt anyone," he would say, and with his big, healthy family growing up there was hard work enough, and plenty of it.

Lou and Rose Harmon were good Catholics, and they were raising their family to have faith in the "Big Boss" upstairs. The "Boss" had treated the Harmons with great generosity in the past years, and they felt they were a lucky couple. When Lou Harmon had courted the young school teacher, Rose Marie Quinn, back in Illinois, he had little of worldly value to offer her. But he was strong, and as a farmer he knew just about all there was to know about the soil and about crops. When the day came for their marriage Rose Marie was nineteen and Lou was only five years older. But they were full of faith and love and had confidence that theirs was bound to be a happy union.

It was about fourteen years later that the first real disaster came and that a real test was put to this young couple. Early in their marriage their first child was born. It was a boy and they named him LaGore. When he was twelve years old he was thrown from a horse. His foot caught in the stirrup and the runaway horse dragged him for more than five miles. LaGore's loss must have been a hard blow. But Mother and Father Harmon knew it was God's will that LaGore should leave this world, and they never thought of having lost their son but only of having turned him over to his Heavenly Father.

A short time later, the family moved from Illinois to Indiana.

Rensselaer wasn't a big town. The people were friendly, and Lou Harmon had a chance to go into business there. The Harmons made friends fast, and it wasn't long before they were firmly established as good citizens of the town. You could always find them in Church on Sunday, and as a general rule Mother Harmon attended daily mass at six o'clock. She still holds to that schedule, and as far as I can remember she has never missed. There are many devout Catholics, but few whose devotion surpasses that of Rose Marie Harmon.

The Harmon family kept on growing and now there were five children, two girls and three boys. Sister Sally was the oldest and the true guiding influence of the rest of the kids. The family was Irish from the word go, and that meant stormy temperaments. There were fights as a general rule, not only when an addition to the family was about due, and if a fight couldn't be worked up at home an outside battle could always be found. The Harmon children felt it was their right to say anything they pleased about each other, but let an outsider make a smarty remark about one of them and the battle royal was on. So far as sticking together goes, the Harmon kids made glue look like weak paste. They just stuck together naturally.

On September 28, 1919, the entire household was unusually quiet. Lou Harmon had gone for the doctor. Harold, Louis Jr. and Gene were hoping the new arrival would be a boy because they felt a little sister would be much harder for them to handle. Sally and Mary Kay had no preference, but they too were pink with excitement at the thought of a new baby, either kind. The doctor arrived and disappeared upstairs. After what seemed like a month of Sundays he emerged with the announcement that it was a fine seven pound boy. Mother Harmon had come through the ordeal like the champion that she was, and everything was in fine shape.

Now the big problem was a name for the new son. Mother and Father Harmon had decided on Thomas for the first name, but they hadn't made up their minds about what to put in the middle.

It was here that Sally came out with a preference and her wish was granted. At this time Sally was going with a boy by the name of Dudley Sands, and she thought Dud, as everybody called him, was a great lad. So at Sally's request the last of the Harmons was named Thomas Dudley.

Having a hand in naming her new baby brother evidently overcame Sally's last reservation about the whole project, for she took on the job of watching over him with enthusiasm. It was sort of a joke that Sally, the only one who had objected to his coming, should be the one who was his special friend.

It seemed that no new arrival could possibly have got a bigger and warmer welcome anywhere.

The first three years of Thomas Dudley's life went by and didn't make much of an impression on him, at least not as far as I can remember. All I have to report about him at that tender age are a few family stories that I got second hand.

When Tom was about three years old he was given a collie puppy, and a truly inseparable friendship grew up between the two. The dog was named Bob, and whether Bob followed Tom like Mary's little lamb or whether Tom followed Bob, one sure thing was that the two of them could get into plenty of trouble. Bob's presence anywhere was a sure-fire indication that young Tom was in the immediate vicinity. All the boys had a lot of fun with the big dog, and it was a familiar sight in Rensselaer to see the Harmon tribe sprinting along the street with Bob enjoying the run as much as any of them.

Tom started to have the wanderlust early in life. He started getting lost early in life too. For his excursions, young Tom had two buddies who lived across the street. Their names were Eddie Smith and Hank Hoover. This trio set out several times to see the wonders of the town, always of course accompanied by their good friend Bob. .

The old-timers around Rensselaer still remember the day when the courthouse was upset by one exuberant collie dog and three youngsters in somewhat unconventional attire. The boys had come down to the courthouse in the course of their explorations, and while there had felt the call of nature. They succeeded in answering the call, but doing up the flaps on the back of their little coveralls again was too much of a tactical problem. The afternoon's play couldn't be stopped just because a mere behind or two was in evidence. The boys just continued to play, flaps down. Nobody could catch them, either.

It was a hurried call that Mother Harmon received on the telephone that afternoon, telling her that her little boy was causing a riot on courthouse square. That wasn't quite the end of the episode. A good week elapsed before Tom's little bottom resumed its natural color.

Early in life, Tom had heard about the Church, and he had often accompanied his parents to mass. As yet he was too young to become a member of the Church, for he had not reached the age of reason. But he was curious, and one bright summer day he and big Bob decided to invade the Church and see what it was all about. When Tom didn't get home for lunch, his mother was a bit anxious, so the family started out to find the lost son. They hunted and hunted, but Tom was in none of his favorite hideouts. Finally brother Gene noticed the big collie outside the church. He was sitting on his haunches with his nose tightly pressed against the crack of the door. This was something more than a clue, and Gene found young Tom inside the church, thor-

4

oughly investigating everything to see what made it tick. Mother Harmon said it showed some sense, anyway, that he had made the dog stay outside.

When Tom was five years old, Father Harmon began to think seriously about the advantages of the steel town of Gary, Indiana, which was located about sixty miles north of Rensselaer. Sally had already got a job there as a secretary at the Gary Bridge Works, and it was money from Sally's earnings that was putting Harold through Purdue University.

It had been agreed among the children that each would help to put the next one through college, and Sally offered to sacrifice her college education so the plan could start with a little principal. This plan was to work out fine, and all the kids except Sally went to college. If ever there came a time when one of the gang was in a tight financial spot, everyone pitched in and took care of it. The old Harmon habit of sticking together really got results.

It was because of Sally that the family decided to move to Gary. Gary was a lively town and the mills were seeking men for all types of jobs. So Lou Harmon thought there would be more opportunity there. It meant giving up friends and associations that had been built up over many years, but it was a move for the better and meant a chance for a steady income.

Sally had been in Gary long enough to know the town and was able to find a home for the family that was close to the school and the shopping district. It was a large house, and Mother Harmon felt that she could aid the financial cause by taking in a boarder or two, especially since the older children were growing up and Harold was away at college. Dad Harmon got a job as a mill policeman, and the family started to make Gary their home.

Life on Jefferson Street was a real merry-go-round. We had a boarder named Harold Knowles whom the family had known in Rensselaer. He was called Knowlsie by all of us, and we thought him one of the finest men on earth. Knowlsie had a great sense of humor, and the person who bore the brunt of most of his jokes was Mary Kay.

Mary was an avid bookworm and always seemed to be tangled up in a mystery story. She did most of her reading in the evening, and often when she thought she was all alone and was deep in some exciting whodunit, Knowlsie was waiting to play a prank on her. One of his favorite tricks was to tie a bolt on a string and dangle it out the upstairs window, letting it tap softly on the window below, near which Mary was sitting. The spooky rapping, on top of the spooky stuff she was reading, was enough to send Mary screaming to her room.

With Mary and Bud in high school and Sally still at home, the house was always full of people of all ages. Mouse, as we called Harold at home, was about to graduate from Purdue, and Mary was all set to go to Butler the following year.

Two older sisters at home with their dates always calling for them meant that Tom was able to work up quite a lucrative business, the sort of juvenile blackmail that young brothers have traditionally levied on their sisters' admirers. He could be harder to get rid of than the measles.

It was also during this period that Bud and Gene managed time and again to send the household into a state of delirium with their teasing of Tom. One of the things they liked to do was to stand him in the middle of the room and say, "Let's see how loud you can yell." Tom would let out a shriek that would have put any first class ghost to shame, but the older boys would blandly pretend it was so weak they couldn't even hear it. Tom would redouble his efforts and yell again and again until he was hoarse. The girls' boy friends got quite a laugh out of this, but whether it was because they thought it was funny that a kid so young should have a voice that sounded like a fog horn on a river boat, or whether they were just glad to see somebody putting one over on young Tom, I wouldn't know.

The time came for Tom to start to school. He was sent to the Holy Angelus School and was taught the three R's there by nuns, for the family frankly believed it would take the patience of a nun (if not a saint) to hammer anything into his head.

The Harmon boys were all interested in athletics, and it was a great day for Tom when Mouse brought him a real football from Purdue. Bud and Gene played a lot of football, and Tom tried to tag along every time. They had a terrible time getting rid of him whenever they wanted to go anywhere. The only sure-fire method was to buy him off with a dime. That was hard-earned money and had to be wisely invested. It generally paid for a movie on Saturday afternoon, usually a horse opera, preferably one with Tom Mix for a hero. At one time Tom (that is Tom Harmon, not Tom Mix) talked his leg off about the "Ace of the Cactus," which was one of his favorites, and it was from this that Bud tacked the nickname "Ace" on him.

Business was not always good. It happened quite often that no dimes were to be had, and then the boys had to let Tom play football with

6

them. He always got his ears belted in, but he was busy learning a lesson or two, especially the lesson of how to take it. The older boys were not very big, but they were big enough to make mince-meat out of their younger brother and they did just that. Tom learned plenty about sportsmanship in those sandlot football games.

Where there is football, there ought to be a clubhouse. Whose idea it was to build one I don't know. Maybe it's just a matter of instinct that boys at a certain age always build a clubhouse. Anyway, the Harmon boys built theirs in the backyard. They made a regular little house out of a number of large packing crates. It had glass windows, hand-made furniture, and best of all, a trap door with a secret passage leading to the front lawn of the Harmon home. It was a swell deal and was used as a meeting place for all the boys of the block. It took some pretty anxious coaxing on Tom's part to be admitted to the fellowship, but admitted he was. It made him feel like a full-sized member of the Jefferson Street gang.

One evening the boys from Adams Street came over and burned down the clubhouse. They just burned it down.

Now, of course, if ever there was a gang of peace-loving youngsters, we were it. But this was too much. What could we do? There was only one clear move—to declare war on those yellow incendiaries. And that was what we did. A formal declaration of war was drawn up and delivered, for all this happened long ago and the simplified method of starting wars which seems to be in use now had not as yet been invented.

The next three days were spent in general mobilization. Both our side and the enemy gathered all the garbage that could be found. The alleys were swept clean, and various storekeepers were asked to do their bit. The following Saturday was D-day. At noon the first shot was fired. It was a fiery red tomato and was heard, if not around the globe, at least around the alley. Now the battle was joined. It went on all day with many a rotten potato changing hands repeatedly. Toward evening Gene upset the whole applecart. He saw something moving in one of the back doors across the alley and let go with a corn cob. It was a good shot, and the cob sailed straight to the mark. It landed right on the nose of one of the boys' father. A deep masculine shout of rage, and both our side and the enemy scattered quickly; no one was caught by the angry parent. The police were called, but they were not very fast in getting there, and the fight flared up again in another

7

sector. Glancing down the alley, you might have thought that a cyclone had gone through it. It was really quite a battlefield.

I had been in the thick of it all day, but I was still ready for plenty more. It was getting late when I stood in the driveway at the rear of the city library, a tomato in one hand and a cauliflower in the other, both ready to be delivered at a moment's notice. It was quite a shock when a large hand reached down from the rear and grabbed my shoulder. In one movement of quick defense against the enemy, I whirled and "smack!" went the tomato. It landed square in a police officer's face with something between a thud and a splash. At the same moment I realized who it was I had hit, and I felt as if something had hit me too, right in the pit of the stomach. In about the same amount of time it had taken me to deliver the tomato, which was not much, the officer had me in the patrol car. My buddy, Eddie Coffehouse, was picked up along with me and together we rode off to jail. To be a real, tough guy you were not supposed to talk, not even to give your name, so I bit my lip and kept mum. I had never been so scared in my life. I knew that Gene, who had been the cause of the cops being called, had gone home and was probably safely in bed. Mom and Dad probably thought he was a little angel. That was a bitter thought.

We sat in police headquarters for about two and a half hours, with a police sergeant for company. The sergeant paid no attention to us. We wanted desperately to see our mothers and tried desperately not to show it.

It was "Dutch" who finally received the call from the police station saying that we were in the hoosegow and wanted to be picked up. He was an old Dutchman who lived with us at that time. He had worked on the farm for Dad's father, and for him the sun rose and set in the younger Harmons. He made a beeline for the police station after that call, and the language he used on the police would have made any Professor of Profanity proud. The episode was over, but it was a very sober Tom who went home with old Dutch that night.

While I was still in grade school, making life miserable for the good nuns of Holy Angelus, the first Harmon left home for good. Sally was secretly married to Bert Jensen, a secret that so annoyed me and so hurt my pride when it became known that I would not speak to Sally for well over two months. The fact that Sally could have something important in her life from which I was excluded wasn't too easy to take.

But school went on, and the recess periods, which were given over

8

to football, handball or baseball, seemed to be much more interesting than anything going on in class. The field at the school was made of cinders, but the boys didn't mind it a bit. Playing on a hard surface was good training. The school was fine, and I am thankful for my association with the nuns who gave me my early training. I probably caused them more trouble and worry than any other five boys, but when I came home from college my first visit was with the nuns who had taken me in hand as a youngster.

When I reached the fifth grade, life seemed to brighten up. My brother Bud got me selected as mascot for his amateur basketball team. Needless to say, it was a great team. I was the happiest kid in school when I trotted out on the floor with the "Kreitzman Treasures." It was quite a task to get that ball all the way up to the basket, but I had loads of fun. Mom had made me a little red sweat-suit and a regulation basketball suit, and this added to my pride. The team won the divisional championship and went to the state tournament at Indianapolis. I could not go because I was not allowed to stay out of school, and when the team lost I was convinced it was because I had not been there to spur them on.

From basketball we went on to baseball and football. Athletics had become my prime interest in life. I guess it was here that my brothers' training began to count, for I loved the thrill of contact, of being socked and socking back. Nothing gave me a better feeling than a hard block or tackle.

At last the great day of graduation came. I could not continue in a Catholic school, since there was no Catholic high school in Gary, and I was sorry to leave the nuns who had done so much for me. The family moved to Pierce Street at this time, so I went to the Horace Mann High School. I have many happy memories of my school days there. I thought I was a tough kid when I came from Holy Angelus, but I soon found out that I was just a soft touch. I went out for football, and the first night at practice I was told to turn in my suit for chewing bubble gum while the coach was talking. I refused, and the coach really had it in for me as a consequence. That coach was Doug Kerr, and he later became one of the greatest influences in my life. After he let the varsity bat me around for my freshman year we got along fine, and it was always to Doug that I went for counsel on my problems.

My high school football career was great experience. I had a wonderful time in school, and felt very proud that the football team won the state championship in our senior year. We had lost eight straight in our freshman year, so the championship of our senior year was quite a change. I also played basketball and ran on the track team. Aside from athletics, my main interest was in dramatics and speech. All in all my life was that of a normal high school boy—sports, dances, and first sweethearts.

Also for the first time I had gained quite a bit of local publicity on the football team. I didn't deserve it more than my teammates, but I was the lucky guy who got to run the ball over the line. As a team, our football lineup at Horace Mann was exceptional, and our coach was as fine a coach as ever there was. Doug Kerr had had his losses in the past, but he finally brought together a bunch of boys who would play ball with him and for him. The team that resulted was a natural, and as a result it had greatness.

The days following high school were the toughest of my life up to then. I was ready to go to college, and Mother and Dad Harmon were making every sacrifice to see that I had everything it was in their power to give me. I made a solemn resolution that I would work as hard as possible so that some day I could repay them for all the kindness and understanding they were giving me. As usual, I knew I had my folks behind me in whatever decision I made, but deciding which college to go to was a tough problem. Mom and Dad listened to all the good and bad points of all the schools considered, but never once did they raise their voices in favor of one school or another. They felt the decision was mine and they left it up to me.

Mouse and Bud had graduated from Purdue, and Gene was attending Tulane. It was after much deliberation that I chose Michigan. Scholastically Michigan is a good school, and on the athletic side it is a member of the Big Ten, so I knew it had everything I wanted.

Another important period in my life was about to begin, and with the faith of my folks behind me I knew I couldn't fail.

MICHIGAN

2

THREE BOYS FROM Horace Mann started out for the University of Michigan together, and believe me it was a great day for the trio. Ray Dwyer, the state champion backstroke swimmer, was one of my companions, and Bill Geisert, one of the most popular boys in high school, was the other.

Michigan wasn't an entirely strange place to me, for I had accompanied Doug Kerr up there to a football clinic once. Doug was a Michigan man and thought a lot of his alma mater.

The school looked wonderful the day we got there. Even today I believe that Ann Arbor in the fall is the most beautiful town in the world, and I have seen a few other beautiful towns since that day. It would take something pretty good in the line of description to tell what Ann Arbor looked like to us that September. The air seemed sort of golden, and the quiet college streets with their big trees were waking up from the drowsy summer as the students began to arrive. The country around the town rolls a little, and the campus is set in the middle like a medallion. I don't know how to say it, but the fact is that Ann Arbor in autumn is *it*.

I was full of anticipation as I went out for freshman football. Forest Evashevski was one of the first guys I met; in the later days of our football career we were to become as important to each other as our right arms. The boys on the Frosh squad made up quite a team. We played the Varsity twice that year, and though I suppose they weren't putting out everything they had, we felt pretty good about beating them both times.

As for my studies, they were getting more than a little tough. I picked up a low grade in one of my courses and would have been ineligible for the coming season had I not been a freshman. So at least I had another season to straighten that out. Things seemed to go wrong all at once; as usual, bad luck didn't come singly. Harry Kipke, who was the coach of the football team, was let out of the university. I had a great respect for Kip, and his going seemed to knock my world topsyturvy. Life seemed a heavy load just then. I was deathly afraid of not making the grade, and of what my family and friends would think if I didn't. But since my folks had placed all their faith and confidence in me I knew I had to make good.

I buckled down to business the second semester. Spring came, with final exams, and I made up my mind to stick out the old chin and go in swinging. I really put forth an effort. The grades came in and everything was great again, for I had made up my deficiency and was in the clear. Another piece of news was that Herbert Orrin "Fritz" Crisler had taken over the reins as football coach, and after meeting him I knew he was as great a guy as was rumored.

In my first year at Michigan I met many fine people, and some of them became life-long friends. One of the landmarks of Ann Arbor is a college bookstore run by Florence Slater. To the athletes at the University Mrs. Slater is a guiding spirit throughout their years at school. Her friendship and encouragement were among the main reasons I stuck it out when I was just about ready to throw in the towel.

At the beginning of every term, Slater's Bookstore is always jammed with students getting set with textbooks for the semester's work. The boys behind the counters handing out those heavy tomes are mainly boys from the different teams. It was always a strange sight to walk into Slater's during or shortly after registration and see a bunch of clerks whose towering size made them look like men from Mars. Just picture one of those giants handing down, all the way down to some pint-sized coed, something or other like the History of Ancient Greece or an anthology of modern French poetry! You could have thought the Michigan teams were the most literary teams in the world. Anyway, Slater's became the hangout of our team. You could always find the majority of the boys of the squad gathered there for a post mortem of Saturday's game, replayed among the textbooks Monday afternoon. The arguments that grew out of these discussions echoed all up and down State Street, the main drag of the college end of town.

One of the prominent figures in these discussions was Professor Art Van Duren, who was always right in the middle of things. He teaches German in the university and also handles the job of being councillor of the underclassmen. A good-humored, casual-mannered exterior hides a lot of real wisdom in Art Van Duren, and he has kept more kids in school with timely advice and help than any other five men in the university put together. His genuine interest and knowledge about sports made him a real friend to the boys around Slater's, and it was to him or to Mrs. Slater that I took my troubles when the going got a little tough. Another good pal of those times is Russ O'Brien, now Sergeant O'Brien, who used to be on the staff at Slater's. This big Irishman is one of the finest friends I made at Michigan.

These people never failed each other, and Slater's is still the gathering place of any of the old gang when they come home nowadays. The discussion and the discussers are both somewhat different—the discussion is all about how to win the war instead of how to win Saturday's game, and the guys deep in argument about it are in uniform instead of the old campus flannels.

At the end of my freshman year I was quite happy when I headed home for my job as a life guard at the Gary beach. In my first year away from home I had tangled with my first adverse criticism and had come out okay. It was a good lesson, for it taught me that if you keep heart and have faith you are bound to come out on top. Looking back on these happenings, even though they seem small now, I know I learned a great deal from my various little upsets.

The job at Gary beach was fine on all accounts. It kept me in the sun all day and gave me an opportunity to build up the strength of my legs. We killed the extra time we had on dull days playing touch football and running in the sand, which is the sort of thing that increases your wind endurance. After a few weeks, though, the summer seemed to drag, and I was anxious to get back to school. I thought over some of the things that stood out in my memory about my first year there. The main thing was the spirit of the students. I don't know how to describe it. I know that people will think I am prejudiced when I say that Michigan has a little something that other universities lack, but to me it is true. There is a sort of zip to the way they get behind their teams, and the big rallies before football games are something worth remembering.

I especially thought of the rally before the Michigan-Michigan State game during my freshman year. The students were really cheering for a win then, for Michigan hadn't looked too good the year before and they wanted to see their faith in their team vindicated. Spirits ran so high that there was a riot of sorts before the game, and I was unintentionally mixed up in it. It didn't amount to very much, but it showed how deep a feeling there was on campus about that game.

The next day the team got beaten by one touchdown, and you might think the students would have been downheared. But not they! They came right back with a bigger pep meeting than ever before the next game, packing Hill Auditorium in a frenzy to tell the team they were behind them more than ever. That was the kind of student body I knew was pulling for me and the other boys of Michigan teams, and it really meant something to us. I am sure the other fellows felt the same as I did, that we absolutely had to be in the best possible condition in order to live up to the loyalty of such a school.

Fritz Crisler was a coach who demanded that you be in top physical condition if you were to play on his team, and no effort was too great for us to make the grade. It was with all these things and a lot more in mind that I returned to the university for my sophomore year and my first varsity competition.

After the first few days of practice, Coach Crisler placed me in the blocking back position. I was bitterly disappointed, as I couldn't see any reason for this move. All through my years in football I had played the running back position, and I couldn't help feeling that I was being pushed around somewhat. Since that time I have learned enough to know that Coach Crisler's reasoning was faultless, but it was certainly not clear to me in the early days of my second year. I was determined to make the grade, and I knew it wouldn't be any cinch because there were some great players on that team. I finally came around to the idea that I didn't care what position I played so long as I could play for Michigan.

The day came for the opening game against Michigan State. Michigan was ready. Fritz Crisler had the team in perfect physical condition. Ray Roberts was the team's trainer. He was the boss of those exercises we went through every night, and thanks to him our team was second to none as far as pure physical fitness was concerned. The morning before the opening game seemed long as it always does, but eventually the team members were in the locker room and the game was about to start.

I had worked hard on my position and hoped to win a starting berth. I was sitting on the end of the bench when Coach Crisler called out someone else to start the game at right halfback, my position. My hopes were dashed, and I took it as a personal defeat. I warmed the bench until a few seconds before the first half was over, and when I finally did get in I was so anxious that I fell all over myself and managed to be more of a detriment than a help to my teammates. However, after I had cooled down things began to work right. We won the game. I couldn't help feeling that I had contributed a little to our success, but whether I was right in that or not, it made me feel quite happy. The second game came up and I started at right halfback. I guess I was the proudest guy on earth. I was still blocking, but I was playing, and that was all that mattered.

We went right through the season like a charm until the Minnesota game. That one was a heart-breaker. We lost it to the tough Swedes of the North by a score of 7 to 6. I was the one who fumbled the ball. Minnesota recovered it, and the following plays led to their touchdown. It was my fault. I had lost that game and nobody else. I swore then that I would avenge the defeat, but I was never able to do it.

After the season was over and I had time to think things out, I could see the logic in Coach Crisler's decisions about me. When I had re-

The Harmon family: (seated, l. to r.) Mary Kay, Dad, Mom, Sally; (standing, l. to r.) Gene, Tom, Bud, Harold.

ported to Michigan for football, I had carried along a lot of advance publicity. I had never given it a second thought, but the fact is, publicity alone can't get you very far. It may give the public the impression that a certain player is good, it may even make the player himself think he is good. But in Big Ten football the fellow playing tackle on the opposing team isn't at all impressed by anything the papers are saying. He isn't going to let you get by just because some sportswriter in the bleachers says you will get by. He isn't going to let anybody get by if he can help it. Really, a fellow who believes that publicity is the finest thing in the world ought to try living on a diet of raw newspapers. He will soon find out that a lot more is needed to keep going and to come out on top. Take my case, for instance. I had come to Michigan to set the world on fire, according to what the newspapers had to say about me. It was impossible to stop them and so I just had to try desperately to live up to the reputation the sportswriters had made for me. As a result, I was pressing, and I was no good at all. Coach Crisler naturally saw all this. He very calmly placed me in the blocking back position, and didn't start me in the first game but let me warm the bench for a while instead. The bench is a great leveller. He started a veteran in the first game because he knew I was ripe to fumble my head off, that is if it would come off. I probably would have gotten it loose if I had played long enough in that first game against Michigan State.

It made me feel better that my family came up for every game they could. We had a great time at football games, and it was a fine thing to have the Harmon clan together again for a while, cutting up as always. Gene was in his senior year at Tulane, and Mouse was down in Gadsden, Alabama. So two members of the family were missing, but otherwise the whole tribe was usually present, and that, by the way, made it much easier for me not to take the newspapers too seriously. If I had ever entertained any ideas of being great like the sportswriters said, the Harmons would have been certain to take the wind out of my sails. In my presence they would never dish out any compliments on my playing, although they may have let fly with a few when I wasn't around. That was the procedure with all the kids in the family, for we didn't want anybody to get to thinking he was too good.

Except for football games, the family was seldom together. The boys all worked in different towns, and Christmas was the one time of year when everybody made an effort to get home for one of Mother Harmon's famous fried-chicken dinners. On Christmas special attention was always devoted to deflating anybody's ego, especially mine.

Every member of the family always got two presents. One present was bona fide, and the other was a gag. It was invariably connected with some outstanding error committed during the previous year by the person who received it. The Christmas after my sophomore year, sister Mary and Jimmy, her husband, gave me a very special present —a football with handles on it. A useful little gadget! That Minnesota fumble was never forgotten. After that whenever I have felt like losing my head and making some kind of a fumble in life, the word "handles" has always popped into my head. I just say "Handles!" to myself and cool down.

The next Christmas, the family gave me an old bird cage. Inside it was a card with a promise: "Next year you get the BIRD." They were pretty simple methods of telling us off in a joking way, but they always worked. Sister Sally was one of the main sufferers. She had wanted a watch for years, and every year the wags of the family would present her with a watch with one part missing—one year it came without a stem, the next year minus the minute hand, and so on. Christmas was always really merry with a succession of gags and jokes.

Outside of the family, I always had Forest Evashevski to contend with. Evy, in my opinion, is one of the greatest guys on earth. As far as playing football goes, I could have run all afternoon in the bathtub and never touched the sides if it hadn't been for him. He smacked them so hard on blocks that you could practically hear them ring. Evy had a great many cohorts, and they were always on hand to see that I never stepped out of line. The teamwork of the football team during my junior and senior years at school was great, and boys like Forest Evashevski, Ed Frutig, Paul Kromer, Ralph Fritz, Al Wistert, Bob Westfall and the rest were all champions at their positions. Their friendship meant more to me than anything else on earth. The newspaper boys were in there trying to build me up, but I couldn't have made second base if the team hadn't been in there functioning like greased lightning. A lot of times I was actually just the lucky guy whose job it was to carry the ball.

The memories of those years at Michigan are the happiest of my life. At the end of the 1940 season, Coach Crisler said: "The team this past year was the greatest team I ever coached, and the craziest." Anybody who knew those boys would have got Fritz's point.

The most important thing with any team is for the players to be in exactly the right frame of mind as they go into the game. In the fine art of bringing his boys up to that pitch, Coach Crisler is a master. On the way to the game he would talk about winning this Saturday, and it would nearly drive him crazy when he found out that the boys in the next car had gone into a huddle on the subject of what they were going to do after the game. How could you get a bunch of guys up to pitch who stood around cracking jokes about Saturday night instead of Saturday afternoon?

Evy and the rest of the boys saw to it that I was the brunt of their jokes. I was a natural for it, getting all that publicity, and being sort of a serious type of guy anyway. In New Haven one night before we were to play Yale the next day, the team was lined up in front of a show. Coach Crisler always took us to a show before the games when we played out of town. It was part of the routine. We were waiting for the manager to get tickets when a bunch of little colored kids came up and recognized the team. The little boys went up and down the line scanning the faces of the players and asking "Where's Harmon?" When they came around, everyone would point towards the end of the line, or else just behind him. I did the same, of course. Evy was in front of me and Ed Frutig behind me. We were clowning along in great style when one of the little boys stopped and said, "There, that's Harmon, sure it is, can't you tell by the nose?" Evy and Frutig never got over that. On various tense occasions in the huddle, Evy would say, "Okay, Harmon, let's get going, get out from behind that nose and ramble!"

The team was always clowning and joking, but when game time came they were always ready.

My junior year we had one swell team. I had worked again during the summer as a life guard at Gary and was in excellent physical shape, looking forward to a good season. Once again we were given the once over by Coach Crisler, and once again we were worked to death for the sake of conditioning. Earl Martineau, the backfield coach, was a great friend of mine and watched out for me as though I were his own son. In practice, we would always start out raising the roof with Bennie Oosterbann and Clarence Munn, the end and line coaches respectively. Everybody had a great time letting out their high spirits. Then Coach Crisler would come out on the field and from then on, it was strictly work.

That was 1939, and the team played great ball. We thought of nothing but football. We were undefeated until we went to Champaign to

Michigan vs. Michigan State, with Harmon—number 98 — going through behind his interference.

tangle with Illini. That was a bitter cold day for Michigan, for although Illinois had not won a game that season they beat us and beat us soundly. We had no excuse. We had played good ball, but the way they were going that day Illinois could have beaten Notre Dame and Minnesota along with us on that gridiron.

The Michigan team took the defeat very hard. Coach Crisler was plenty worried because we were to play Minnesota the following week and we knew that would be a tough one. It is a startling thing to see boys who are football players and are tough as iron crying like babies, but that was what happened after that Illinois game. You get keyed up to such a pitch for a game that a let-down like that is terrific. I felt ashamed to go back to school and face the students, and I know that the rest of the team felt the same way. If we could have gone and buried our heads somewhere for a while we would have done it.

As was expected, we failed to bounce back for the following Saturday, and Minnesota really gave us a trouncing. These were the only two games we lost that year, and the mixed-up final results were sort of ironical. We had beaten both Ohio State and Iowa, the two great teams that wound up in first and second place in Big Ten standings, and they had licked both the teams that got the better of us.

The season was over, and instead of looking back we were looking forward to the next season. Most of the boys were going to return and we could be sure of having a great team again. Evy was elected Captain, and that was all we needed. He was one of the smartest boys I have ever known. He never knew what the word defeat meant and was always in there fighting until the end.

I had been selected on the All American teams, but it seemed more like a token honor to me, for I felt that the whole team deserved it if I did.

School was going on as usual, and we never quite forgot the books during our heavy work with football. Topics were still being talked over in the back of Slater's bookstore. There was a new one now, one we didn't know much about, but that only made arguing the easier. The fellows didn't seem to think the war in Europe would affect them for some time, for we all felt sure that the United States would stay out of it this time. The draft was only starting and wouldn't get to us for some time. The draft was only defensive, anyway. What had we gained out of World War I but a lot of bad debts? Hadn't it been the war to stop wars? It hadn't succeeded, and why should we get into an-

20

other one? That is the way we were thinking in those days, so far away now.

I felt about the same as everyone else. I wasn't worried about the war very much. After all I had final exams coming up soon, and to me those grades were more important than Hitler taking care of Poland. It was with little realization of what was to come in a few years that I went along merrily and earnestly on my way through school.

Professor Van Duren was always in on these conferences, not trying to run them but putting in a lot of information and wisdom about the past experiences of our country. I am sure he realized that every one of the boys sitting there arguing would be in the middle of the mess before it was over. But Slater's was still Slater's, and war or no war we were still in college and we stood our ground. It wasn't our mess, or so we thought. If Hitler started for America we would take care of him, that was understood, but until that time arrived we had more important business to attend to. That feeling was almost to cost us this wonderful country of ours, but we couldn't see it that way then.

It was summer before we realized it. Spring in Ann Arbor had been as beautiful as ever, but spring is the season when college boys and girls have their examinations to worry about, and that feature tended to blind us somewhat to the extraordinary beauty of our campus. Once exams were over, life appeared very rosy to me. I had finished three years at Michigan, and had just one more to go. The friendships I had made were the best in the world, and I felt I had gained a lot from my studies. My grades were good, and I had a job for the summer, my usual swell job at the beach. I would practice outdoors and look forward to the next football season and my senior year.

We had lost all our kickers on the football team by graduation that spring, and I was determined to get in trim to take over the kicking job. I practiced on the beach with the rest of the boys, and really got into the best physical shape ever.

One of the best friends I had made when I started in school at Michigan was Dr. Harry L. Cooper. Dr. Cooper was and still is one of the most enthusiastic Michigan men in existence. His judgment in all matters of life, including football, was seldom wrong. I looked up to his experience, and he took a great interest in me. I considered him practically a second father. He never missed a Michigan football game, and since he was always on deck with the Harmons after the game he and Mrs. Cooper got to be considered as part of the crazy Harmon clan. Now Mom and Dad Harmon were not in the best of health, and after consulting Dr. Cooper about it I decided that I would take Mom on a trip to the West that summer before returning to Ann Arbor.

Mother had relatives in South Dakota, and my college sweetheart lived in Wyoming. I had always wanted to see the West and felt this was as good a time as any. I asked permission to have two weeks off before the end of the bathing season, and the leave was granted. Mom and I drove together to South Dakota. We wanted to have Dad come along with us, but his job couldn't take care of itself, so he had to stay at home and work. It was the first time in my life that I did all the sponsoring of anything for Mother and Dad, and it made me very happy. Mom had a swell time, and I enjoyed myself too. I think seeing the pleasure and happiness in Mom's face was the finest thing of the whole trip to me. The change had done her a world of good, and I was now more than ever determined to do my best to see that she and Dad got all the happiness they deserved.

I returned to school for my senior year in fine fettle. The team was going to be wonderful, of that I was sure. Evy, as Captain, had made all the boys sign the pledge. In that pledge we solemnly swore that as members of the squad we would at no time smoke or drink or break training rules. The coaches had nothing to do with that pledge—it was the team's own idea, and we stuck to it. I am sure that was one of the reasons why this turned out to be one of Michigan's greatest teams—and Michigan has had some mighty great teams in its time.

To me training had always been a law. I never broke training during all the time I played for Michigan. It wasn't hard to hold to when football was a matter of life or death to you.

Evy in particular was in wonderful shape and was as inspiring a Captain as could be imagined. The rest of the team was raring to go. We sailed into our schedule and won every game until we came to Minnesota. For every member of the team, the whole season pointed to that one game. The big adversary was Minnesota. We wanted to win that game more than all the others put together. The team was all set for the big struggle, but the morning of the game the worst break in the world happened for the Michigan team. When we got out of bed and looked out the window it was raining. Not just drizzling, but really raining.

This was going to mean a real advantage to Minnesota, for on a muddy field her heavier team would be favored. Extra weight really counts under conditions like that. It didn't stop the boys from Michigan in their fervor to win the game, because they were bound that

Forest Evashevski, captain of the
Michigan team, and Tom Harmon.

come what might it should be our victory that day. We had been waiting a long time for this chance, and today we really felt we were ready to fight and win in spite of everything and anything.

Well, the boys did play a great game, but we lost it. Seven to six. The same score as our sophomore year. It didn't seem possible, but there it was. We had played a great football, our plays had worked swell, but we couldn't seem to work it across the line that counts. It just wasn't in the cards to be our ball game. I don't think that I have ever experienced a greater disappointment in my life. After the game I didn't want to see anyone. I went to the locker room and sat down and cried. We couldn't beat the Swedes and we wouldn't have another chance.

That night, before we boarded the train, I had a quiet supper with Mom and Dad and Doctor and Mrs. Cooper. My spirits had hit rock bottom, but after talking to these four people I pepped up. It was a hard lesson to learn to be a good loser. But we had more ball games and we had to win them.

The team bounced back and won the rest of the games on the schedule. The newspaper boys were laying it on thicker than ever where I was concerned. I tried to tell them that they ought to spread the credit more evenly, for no guy can carry a ball far if the rest of the team isn't in there clearing the way. All my talking did little to change the flood. If I could have had my way, the All American Team of 1940 would have been the Michigan team in toto, and it wouldn't have been a bad All American by a long shot.

Anyway, the publicity didn't make a dent on the boys in the squad, one way or the other. They were continually making fun of the newspapers and their stories. One night when I came out for practice, Bob Ingalls, our center from Marblehead, Mass., said to me quite seriously so I didn't catch on that he was trying to razz me again: "Tom, you are really not the most important guy on this team." You can see how this thing had got me from my silly reply, "I know, Bob, I never said I was."

"Well," Bob went on, "I've been thinking it over, and I've come to the conclusion that I'm the most important guy on this squad myself. I just happened to think the other night, you and the rest of the boys would look awful silly running back there if I never passed the ball."

That was the good-natured attitude of all the boys. They understood what the newspaper stories amounted to and were my friends. They knew it wasn't my doing. I could never have asked to belong to a

24

greater team or a finer bunch of men. I was proud to be associated with them.

* * * * * *

After football was over, the world suddenly seemed very close at hand, and sort of flat. The thought that intercollegiate football was finished for me was hard to get used to.

Of course I had my studies to continue until the end of the year. All my efforts along that line had been pointed for a chance in radio. I knew that my fame as a football player would soon be over, for new guys carrying the ball would absorb the public's attention next season. I had been fortunate enough to win the Heisman trophy and a few other trophies as the football player of the year, but again it was sort of an empty feeling. What I wanted was that little gold football emblematic of the Big Ten Championship, and that was the thing we had not been able to win.

It was a wonderful experience at this time to travel to various cities to receive those football trophies. It gave me an opportunity to meet a great many grand people, and I enjoyed that aspect of it in particular. I now found that, due to all the publicity I had received in my football career, I was in some demand as a speaker. I had majored in speech work all through my studies, and this type of thing would aid me in radio work later and also give me a chance to earn some money on the side. Naturally, I took quite a few of the engagements. Money was coming in, and I was proud to be able to tell Dad that from now on, I could assume some of the responsibilities of the Harmon family. It gave me more satisfaction than anything in the world. I also had to keep working on my studies, for I wanted that diploma like anything.

The schedule for keeping up in the school work and also taking in banquets on the "Lettuce League," as it is known, was a bit tough, but money for Mom and Dad was waiting and that was incentive enough to make me turn handsprings. Later on in the spring I found out that Hollywood wanted to make a picture and were offering me big money to do it. I spoke to the family, and they agreed on the deal, so I went ahead on plans for it. My world had never seemed rosier. We were still not in the war, and I considered Mom's and Dad's welfare as my primary responsibility. Of course I knew that the publicity couldn't help me in keeping a job later on, but it would certainly help in getting one. I started on a royal tour of the banquet circuit.

My appearance as a guest on the Eddie Cantor show hit me like a bolt out of the blue. It was wonderful. Here was I, a punk from a little town, having all these opportunities. It seemed almost like a dream. I was a little nervous before the program, but then the thought crossed my mind: "Brother, do you need handles on this ball?" That made me laugh at myself, and things went off all right.

I was never more thankful to the good Lord above than I was at that time for placing me in a family like mine and giving me the training that I had had in football, for I was certainly not dumb enough to believe that what I had attained was just the result of my own efforts. I knew very well how much I owed to the concentrated work and cooperation of all my friends and teammates. One thing I really minded was being called conceited. Confidence in yourself is one thing, but conceit is another. In a way fame is fine, but it can certainly put a guy behind the eight ball. I only had a little taste of it, but I can well imagine how the really famous people of the world must feel at times. It isn't all roses and sunshine.

The banquets came and went. I was still sticking in school. About a week after the beginning of the second semester, I was called into the office of the Dean. I was told that my school work had been suffering, and if I wanted to graduate I would have to forget about the banquets. I was sorry to have to do that because I had Mom and Dad on my mind and felt they could use the money. However, I wanted that diploma, so I stayed home and only took on engagements at the banquets that were close enough so I could attend them and still not miss any classes. This went along fine for a time.

Then something unexpected and really big took my breath away. I was extended an invitation to the President's Birthday Ball, and also an invitation to have luncheon with the President of the United States at the White House. It was the greatest honor I had ever received or could imagine receiving, but I said I was sorry, I couldn't possibly make it. I guess the Senator on the other end of the wire must have just about swallowed his teeth. Slowly he came to again and said, "My boy, do you realize that this is an invitation from the President of the United States? You can't just refuse that!" I told him that I appreciated the honor but that if I missed a class I would not graduate, and regardless of the great honor of this invitation, I had to get that diploma. He replied that he would talk to a few Senators and that they would talk to the Dean who had me on the carpet.

The Senator called back again and said they had arranged everything. I didn't doubt their word, but I went to see the Dean just for my own satisfaction. He was in conference and wouldn't be out until five o'clock. I had to catch the four o'clock plane if I was going to make the Birthday Ball, so I took off.

The party was a swell one, and meeting President Roosevelt was a great moment in my life. I enjoyed every bit of it, and didn't forget a silent prayer of thanks afterwards to the "Big Boss" upstairs for giving me such an honor.

However, the following morning when I returned to school I was called into the Dean's office. He told me that I was going to be expelled for disobeying orders.

I was so flabbergasted, I didn't think of telling him there must be some misunderstanding. I just didn't know which way to turn. My graduating meant everything in the world to me, and I was sure that if Mom and Dad knew that I wasn't to graduate they would be terribly disappointed. I went to Mrs. Slater's and to Professor Van Duren. I told them all about what had happened. I had only missed one class, and I had secured the permission of the instructor to be absent before I left.

I went to my room that night and felt as if the bottom of the world had dropped right out. What a way for my college career to end! At about eight o'clock one of my speech professors telephoned. He asked me about the rumor that I was being expelled, and I told him it was the truth.

The next day I was called to President Ruthven's office and was told that the matter had been cleared up. I was allowed to stay in school and finish with my classmates. There seemed to be something firm under my feet after all, that old bottom really hadn't fallen out from under my world. Later I discovered that my professor had interceded for me, and that I was found not guilty of letting my schoolwork suffer because of my tours. I felt pretty happy that my professor was in there pitching for me. It was at times like these that I knew and appreciated true friendship.

Graduation time seemed to come up in a hurry. It was a tremendous thrill to see ole Evy leading the class in the senior march, for Evy, besides being Captain of the football team, was also the President of the Senior Class. It was a fine day when we graduated, and when I walked up to the platform for my diploma I felt like a million dollars. Evy was at my side on our last day of school, as he had been so many times on the football field, and that made the ending just right. The family were there too, so I was doubly happy.

Sally and Mary helped me pack after the ceremonies were all over, and I felt a sudden gust of melancholy about college days being at an end. I guess every graduate goes through that moment. I knew I would go on living in Ann Arbor. I had been offered a job at radio station WJR in Detroit and was planning to drive back and forth to work every day, for I had made up my mind that I would build a home for Mom and Dad in Ann Arbor and we would live there together. All that was very nice, but still, it would not be the same.

The movie would help me to pay for the new home, so with that to look forward to we left together for Gary, Indiana, to say goodbye to everyone before I left for the great adventure of Hollywood. I spent about ten days at home before shoving off to meet two of my best pals from school. All three of us were going out to the coast.

Bill Farnsworth was in Springfield, Illinois, and Bones Barnes was to pick him up there. The three of us met at a prearranged place and drove out west together. We had a swell trip. The sights of the Boulder Dam and the Grand Canyon alone were enough to travel for. We arrived in Hollywood, and the first problem was a place to live. Mom and Dad were coming out to visit me, so I rented a small apartment. The three of us had spent the first few days getting acquainted around town. I was scheduled to start the picture the following week, so we used our time while we could to make the rounds. I was looking forward to my parents coming later in the summer, and thought the vacation would do them good.

The picture work turned out to be interesting, and I enjoyed seeing how things work in a movie studio, but the actual picture was Limburger cheese, well done! The title was "Harmon of Michigan," but the picture itself had about as much relation to the reality of my school years as a piggy bank has to a real honest-to-gosh porker. It made quite a bit of money, they said, and I guess that was the main point. I can't imagine the public really liking the show, though, because it was more than I could ask my best friends to stomach. However, I had fun and I was making money for that home for Mom and Dad, so I would have tried to play Hamlet if it had been asked of me.

During the time I was in Hollywood I met a girl. Maybe I should say THE girl. She was in the movies, but it seemed to me that she was a little different from most of the picture girls. She was natural—not that most of the Hollywood Queens are not natural, but this girl

28

seemed to be real and down to earth. Not that most of the Hollywood Queens are unreal—but, anyway, this girl seemed different. I started to have dates with her, and we had great times together. Bones and Bill would corral their dates, and together we would take in dances and parties. I guess one of the biggest thrills was an invitation to a party at Bing Crosby's, for the "groaner" is one of the greatest guys on earth. It was Bing who had got me the chance to make a movie in the first place. The party at Bing's was a big hit. Some of the greatest names in show business were all there in the same room—Bob Hope, Andy Devine, Ken Murray, Phil Silvers, Johnny Mercer and a lot of others. It was quite a thrill for a ham football player to be mixing in this crowd.

More work followed, and finally the picture was finished. I had continued going with Elyse Knox, my swell girl. Bones and Bill and I had nicknamed her Butch early in the game, a comical switch from Elyse, but still it somehow seemed to express how real and true she is. I hated the thought of leaving Hollywood, for we had had a lot of fun together, but I had to return to Chicago to play in the Chicago-All Star game. This game was something I had dreamed about since I was a kid, so I didn't want to be denied the privilege of playing in it. It was especially because of Butch that I hated to leave, so I asked her to come to the game and she said she would. It was a great help to know she would be there.

The Chicago-All Star game was a big thrill. We worked for two weeks and had a fine team, but we were no match for the powerhouse of the Chicago Bears and we lost. It seemed funny that I was playing against the same team that had drafted me in the National League Football draft. I guess there was quite a bit of speculation as to whether or not I would play professional football. I have nothing in the world against the professional sport, but I couldn't see any future in it. I knew that it would be an opportunity to make a great deal of money in a short time, but all the same I knew I would be better off if I started my radio career right away instead of waiting two or three years. I have never been sorry that I made that decision. It would have been a great honor to have played with the Chicago Bears, but it was even more important to get a start in my chosen work.

From the All Star game I went to my job at WJR in Detroit. I was the sports announcer for the station and was very happy with my job. I was broadcasting the Michigan football games, which was quite different from playing in them, but I was associated with sports and was

29

content. It was a steady job and the salary was good. More and more, while on duty at the station, I followed the late war news as it ticked in.

It seemed to me inevitable that the United States would be in this mess before it was over. I wondered where I stood, and knew I had to work it out for myself. If I went, I wanted it to be in the Air Corps. That was the only branch for me. But I also had Mom and Dad on my mind, so for the moment I buckled down to my job and worked as hard as I could.

I finished out the football season broadcasting the games, and then went into the Air Corps. I enlisted on November 8th. It was just one month later that some rats from across the Pacific pulled the dirtiest backstabbing act in history.

I wasn't called up immediately on my enlistment, so I continued to work. Our home in Ann Arbor was finished and I was the proudest man on earth. I certainly hated the thought of leaving my home and my job, but I knew that if enough of our young men were in the Army, not Hitler nor any other power in the world could stand a chance against the United States. I figured that all the other thousands of young men hated to leave home and the ones they loved as much as I did, and we were all to make the same material sacrifice, for the same big cause. I knew it wouldn't be a picnic, but I began to anticipate my call into the Air Corps. It looked like the beginning of a new adventure that would have some valuable experiences in it. I guess my thinking wasn't far wrong. If excitement was what I was looking for, I sure got it—but *good!*

THE AIR CORPS

3

GETTING INTO THE Army Air Corps wasn't an easy job. I thought that I would be called at once, but I was soon to learn differently. It seemed that I wasn't the only American who was raring to join the flying end of our army. I had enlisted in November, and it was the following March before I was called.

The feeling a guy gets from that telegram calling him to duty is impossible to explain. I had been expecting it for so long and had had plenty of time to think of all the possible consequences. But there is quite a difference between a thing like that when you imagine it ahead of time and the shock when it finally arrives. I don't mean to say that I was looking at things at all from a pessimistic viewpoint. In fact, the idea of ducking a bullet or two during my army career didn't really bother me, but it certainly didn't please me either.

I had been living with Mom and Dad in our new home in Ann Arbor for just three months, driving back and forth to Detroit every day. Mom and Dad had made quite a sacrifice in giving up their home and friends in Gary to come and live with me, and I hadn't had as much time as I would have liked to introduce them around. Now that I was leaving they would have to make new friends in Ann Arbor on their own, and I thought that wasn't an easy prospect. When anyone came to the house, I would make him promise to come and see Rosebud and Lou, as all the kids called the folks. I wanted to be sure Mom and Dad would have plenty of company to keep them cheered up after I left. As things turned out, I guess I needn't have bothered. I was calculating without Mom's and Dad's ability to "Meet friends and influence people." They did all right without me.

The night before I was to leave for the Air Corps we had a little going-away party. I think we invited the whole town of Ann Arbor. Everything was fine and we all had a good time. Mom and Dad stuck out the evening with me because it was our last night together. I had to catch a plane at six a.m., so we stayed up all night and talked. After all the people at the party had gone, Mom, Dad, Sally, Mary and I finished up the night. We talked about everything under the sun. I know Mom and Dad must have been a bit worried that night, but they never let it show. They kept up the attitude that I was just going on another trip and would be back soon. As I have often said before, and will certainly say again, nobody else can hold a candle to Mom and Dad Harmon when it comes to stout hearts and chins up. They knew what the war was, but they had undying faith in the good Lord, and if any one factor was responsible for my coming back, that faith was it.

I made my plane and set out for Santa Ana, California. I was happy to be catching the west coast, for I thought it would give me a chance to see some of my friends out there. The Air Corps can't keep you busy all the time, I thought. Well, in that I was slightly off the beam. But anyway, I didn't have to report until Monday morning. This was Saturday. So I went to the home of my old buddy Bill Farnsworth, who had driven out to the coast with me the previous spring. Bill had stayed on there and found a good job in an airplane factory. We had a great reunion. On Monday he drove me over to Santa Ana where we went straight to the administration building. And boy, was I amazed! I never even imagined there were so many soldiers. Some had the look of veterans, but a lot of them looked just as green as I was at that point.

I reported in. A sergeant took my papers and waved me to a tent area. I was in the Army now.

I reported to my tent, and Bill left. I sat down on an empty bed and wondered what to do next. Never in my life have I experienced a feeling of loneliness such as that. But my dejection was short lived. Boys started to come into the tent, and each took possession of an empty bed. I noticed they were all enlisted men who had been selected by the Air Corps the hard way. They had been through basic training and come up through the ranks. We were all given our bedding and so on and were told to make our tents ready. I didn't know the first thing about making a bed army style, so I was in luck to be in a tent with a bunch of experienced old-timers. We all introduced ourselves and got together. The veterans gave the recruits a hand, and did I appreciate it! Uniforms were not passed out as yet, so for about a week we lived in fatigues. Fatigue clothes are fine for hard work, but they are definitely not dressy. I didn't care about that, though, for I knew I couldn't go out for the week end. One of the first things I had learned was that new members of the army are quarantined for thirty days. I didn't mind too much, for I had a lot of work to do. The other boys in the tent had been in the army for long months already and were in no mood for another spell of quarantine. They squawked plenty but it didn't do them much good.

Santa Ana is one of the Army's big pre-flight schools. If California is the land of sunshine, maybe the Chamber of Commerce doesn't consider Santa Ana to be a part of that state. Of the thirty-five days I was at Santa Ana it rained thirty-four. I had never minded rain in the past, but being in the Army and living in a tent was changing my viewpoint on the subject of rain, at least. My opinion was definitely against it. With the rain came mud, as I knew from football days, but football was nothing like this. Everyone who came into the tent brought in a bucket of mud on his shoes, and we had to keep that tent clean. We stood inspection every morning, and that meant a daily scrub job. It didn't do us much harm, but after all, I thought, I had joined the

Army to fly, not to become a certified chambermaid. I sure had a lot to learn!

During the first week I was given instructions by my tentmates in the manual of arms. I kept cracking myself on the head with a heavy Springfield rifle and raising a welt. After a week of the manual of arms as taught by these ex-infantrymen, I was doubly happy that I was in the Air Corps. Lugging that big gun around in the rain or in the hot sun looked definitely a job.

As days went on I began to enjoy the army life. Plenty of times it seemed like a pain, but the calisthenics were getting me in shape again and eating and sleeping on a definite schedule made me feel swell. And it was always great sport to sit in the tent for ten minutes and swap a few yarns with the boys.

During the first two weeks we were kept busy taking tests; these were to determine our kinds of ability in order to have us classified for training as pilots, navigators or bombardiers. We would often re-hash the test we had just taken, and we had great arguments about what the right answer was to such and such a question. As was only to be expected, everybody was shooting for training as a pilot. In a class as large as ours it was obvious that all couldn't be pilots and some would miss out on their choice, although all those boys would do a good job wherever they landed.

My prayers to Saint Anthony and the Blessed Virgin were put on the double those two weeks. I kept trying to convince myself that everything was going okay. But I don't think I felt so very certain about it all, for time and again I caught myself trying to figure out how things would be if I failed to make pilot training. This was only my first experience of "sweating out a deal" in the army. Since then I have worried with the best of them.

It was terrible to be finished with the tests and have nothing to do but wait for the results. Each day a few more boys of our squad would be notified and removed to different barracks, while the rest of us waited. The pilots were housed together, as were the navigators and the bombardiers. It was a case of heavy thinking while you waited to see what you were classified and which barracks you would be sent to. I even got to talking to myself when alone. I argued with myself that no professor could tell if you would make a good pilot just from something you had written down on a piece of paper. I thought that every-one should be given a chance to fly. If he washed out then, well, there was still time for him to become a navigator or a bombardier, and the boy would be satisfied he had had a chance. It would not be as if the boy were put out without even a chance to swing the bat.

I was so wrapped up in the idea of being a pilot that it never occurred to me that there have to be guys to fill all the berths,' and if a person's abilities are more in one line than another he should be put in the berth where he fits best. I figured the tests over and over, I worried more and more, and most of all I prayed. I really wanted that chance.

The day of days came. I can well remember Lieutenant Nelson, my commanding officer, telling me I was wanted in the classification office. A young Captain was at the table. I entered in my best military way, saluted and stood stiffly at attention. The Captain asked me a few questions and then said, "Harmon, you are classified as a pilot." I could have turned a somersault then and there, I was that happy. Instead I saluted, inwardly thanking the "Boss Upstairs" for not letting me down. I thanked the officer and, once outside, ran all the way back to our tent. So far four of us were notified, and so far we had all been classified as pilots. I was happy and relieved. I now resolved to make the grade or bust. I had the chance, and now it was up to me to come across.

After about ten days more of Santa Ana and the mud we heard that the next class was getting set to leave for flying school. We were to be included in this bunch. The last ten days before we left were wonderful days. I had been assigned to Squadron 12, a pilot squadron with a great bunch of boys in it. Our commanding officer was Lieutenant A. Lee Lowery. He went to bat for his men whenever necessary, and in return his men never let him down.

The water fights and pillow brawls were many in the three barracks of Squadron 12, and more often than not Lieutenant Lowery was in the middle of them. One of the favorite tricks of these kind roommates was to tie your bed up to the ceiling and make a million knots in your bed clothes. This was naturally accomplished in the absence of the victim, who was innocently away at a card game or something. The game or whatever it was would of course progress right up to lights out, and the cadet would then come scrambling back to get into his bed before the cadet officer of the day made his bed check. It would be a room full of muffled laughs as the other roommates feigned sleep and smothered their merriment at the poor fellow searching for his bed in the dark, only to find it securely fastened to the rafters.

In all the wonderful memories I have of the Air Forces, the cadet

34

days seem to hold top place for happy times. The high spirits of the boys in the corps made it impossible for any sourpuss to stay that way long. Hazing was still going strong when we were cadets, and an upperclassman could make you feel like small peanuts quicker than you could blink an eye. You might not enjoy the experience at the time, but there was nothing to do about it. The army was built on discipline, and the upperclassmen were sure to see you got plenty of it.

I imagine the number of boys the army makes into real men is pretty big. It made no difference who you were or what your standing had been in civilian life, now you were just one of a whole bunch of aviation cadets and sometimes no station in life could have looked lower to you. According to the standards of rank in the army, you were somewhere between an officer and an enlisted man, but at times the lowliest private made you feel uneasy. Yet you always felt proud of your station, because the men who were aviation cadets today would be the flying officers of tomorrow. The way all cadets felt about it, the day you got your wings you really became a man.

The day came to leave for Primary. It should have been a happy day for me, but on the morning we were to go I received a telegram from Sister Sally. Dad had been taken to the hospital, desperately sick. He was going to have an operation. I went at once to the Chaplain. I felt that my place was at my father's side. I had waited what had seemed a long time to be placed in a class to start flying, but even so I wanted above all to go home. I had a long talk with Father Clasby, the Catholic Chaplain at Santa Ana, whose long experience with the cadets made him a wise and understanding adviser. He said he could get me an emergency furlough if I wished it, but he suggested that I go to my Primary school first, as any delay might mean I would be put back a class or even reclassified. Following his judgment, I went on to the Primary Flying School to which I had been assigned, with my group. It was at Oxnard, California, a school with the reputation of being both good and tough. I was to learn that it held up to its advance billing and then some.

We traveled to Oxnard by train, and in spite of our casual way of taking it, it was an anxious trip for all of us, because we were looking forward so hard to our first chance to fly. I continued to worry about Dad, but once we arrived at Oxnard there was little time for worrying. The school is about thirty-five miles north of Los Angeles, along the ocean; it is a beautiful place. We thought we were quite the boys when we got off the train; coming into the station we had seen the cadets lined up on the platform waiting for us. As we descended we noted the ruler-straight carriage of these cadets. They were dressed in pinks, white shirts, black ties and white gloves. The majority of them wore sabers dangling from their sides. The funny little buttons worn on their shoulders we later found out to be the insignia of Cadet Officers. The minute we got off the train we were told to fall in. Then it seemed that all hell broke loose. The barrage started! It was: "Well, mister, you're at Oxnard, we of Oxnard are proud, suck in that chin! Chest out! Stomach in! How old are you, mister? Okay, let's see you put that many wrinkles in your chin!—What are you, mister, a bird dog? Keep those eyes straight! We are now going to march through the town of Oxnard, and if any one of you sees even a part of the town you'll pay for it. Keep those eyes straight! No bird-dogging! Attention! Left face! Forward march!" With that final command we started through town. The townspeople of Oxnard lined the sidewalks and laughed heartily at the sight of the upperclassmen tearing into the new underclassmen. But to us it wasn't very funny. After a little of it, our tormenters hardly seemed human, and it was as if some hostile force had set upon us determined to make life as miserable as possible. Without thinking about it, I had elected to carry my grip in my hand. It was heavy enough, but by the time I reached the base some six miles from the depot it seemed to weigh a ton. Marching in the hot sun for six miles at strict attention would have been hard enough without baggage, but my suitcase and I stuck in there and so did the two upperclassmen who were on my tail all the way.

If we thought our experience at the depot was bad, we soon found out our error. We hadn't seen anything yet. When we arrived at the gates, the whole upper class was there waiting for us. We got quite a reception. We stood in a circle around the barracks and put wrinkles in our chins and answered "Yessir," until we were blue in the face.

I was right in the middle of it, but I was still worrying about Dad. Finally a Cadet Captain came over to me. I "popped to" and asked if I could ask him a question. He said I could. With that I showed him the telegram and asked him if I might be able to see the Commandant of Cadets about going to my father's side. The atmosphere changed at once and I was whisked to the office of the Commandant. I then explained my situation and all the data was taken down. I would be informed shortly. Hazing might be hazing, but when those boys saw a guy whose father was desperately sick, they wanted to help all they could. The tough attitude ceased and everyone wanted to help me to get home.

However, about nine o'clock that evening I was informed that my emergency furlough had been refused. I was greatly hurt. I didn't realize it then, but what had happened was that the Commandant had wired the Red Cross in Ann Arbor to find out how my father was doing, and the reply that he was "resting easy" had come back. Since he didn't want to see me put back a class, the Commandant refused my leave. It was only with full knowledge of my father's condition that he had reached his decision. Army orders don't come with explanations, but soon I had a long letter from Sister Sally informing me that Dad was coming along fine and not to worry.

We finally got down to work. The schedule that we were given was a honey. It started at five a.m. and allowed not more than a few seconds for catching one's breath before "lights out" at nine every night. You never had to worry about the underclassmen being slow to turn in, not only because we were dead tired but also because those hours in bed were the only ones when the upperclassmen didn't bother us. Sleep was the only refuge we had. The daily schedule started with calisthenics at five, following which we had about fifteen minutes to dress, clean our rooms, have a precision fold in the sheets on our beds, and everything in apple pie order. At first the schedule seemed a little difficult, but by the time we had become upperclassmen we were so proficient that we even had a few minutes free between formations.

The "dodos," as the underclassmen were called, had to go everywhere on the double. We had to "pop to" every time an upperclassman entered our room. The upperclassmen saw to it that we had few free moments. The penalty for any infraction of this discipline or any fault with your dress or your room meant "gigs." "Gigs" are a sort of demerit system. One gig would make it tough for you, and if you had three gigs you would forfeit your week-end pass. Every gig over three had to be walked off at the rate of one hour on the ramp. It made anybody darn sure to watch himself closely! At first, the underclassmen were more than a bit peeved at the upperclassmen, because they felt they were being picked on. It was a natural enough reaction—all underclassmen feel the same way. But there was always the day to look forward to when you yourself would become an upperclassman, and that eased the pain.

Oxnard was a proud school. We were trained to believe that Oxnard cadets carried a mark of distinction with them. And with the training we got a cadet would seem like a different boy by the time he was finished with Oxnard from the one who had arrived fresh from Santa Ana. He had attained a sort of snap that is hard to describe but easy to recognize. Oxnard cadets were proud of their school.

The one place where the upper class had no jurisdiction over us was on the flying line. That first trip to the "flight line" thrilled every one of us past expectation. The line became our haven. We could relax and do as we wished when we were not flying or in conference with our instructors. My instructor was John Canada. He could fly the pants off anything that had wings on it, and if I never remember anything else, I shall always remember the patience with which John Canada handled a certain ham halfback from Michigan. He was a quiet person. His voice was soft, but it wasn't a wise thing to get him riled, for then his eyes could burn with rage. He succeeded in getting me quite sick on our first ride. He asked if I would like to do some spins. I thought I was the toughest guy in the world, nothing could faze me— so Canada began to give me the spin business. I didn't quite toss my breakfast, but I sure felt a nest of butterflies down in the old esophagus. That was my first and only experience with air sickness. I had just enough of it so I can sympathize with all the folks who are afflicted with that mean little malady.

Flying went on, and every day seemed more interesting than the day before. We had a lot of "hot pilots" in the class. Most of these boys had had some flying time before going into the cadets, and they knew their way around a plane.

The time finally came for that first solo flight. Johnny Canada asked me to taxi over to the line, and then he got out of the ship. He said, "Are you ready?" I just about dropped, because at that moment I had no more idea of soloing than of making waffles. But I was determined that if he thought I was ready, I would be. At least that is what I told myself. I crossed my fingers and said "Yup" as confidently as I could, just as though I had been doing this kind of thing every day in the year. I am sure that if anybody in the next county had happened to be listening closely he could have heard a steady thudding noise, the sound of my shaking knees beating a tune on the sides of the plane. I swallowed once, gunned the motor, and then started out for the end of the runway. It sure did look lonely without the instructor up front to help out if you got into trouble. I reached the runway, checked my mags and started into the wind. The ship rose easily and I got into the traffic pattern. I was trying to keep in mind all the million and one things I had learned. "Keep a thousand foot traffic pattern, wings level, nose on horizon, coordinate your turns" and all the other things the instructor had told me. I came around for a landing and was tense as a tennis racket. I started down and everything went fine it seemed until I came to about ten feet off the ground. I had let my airspeed get a little low, and the ship stalled out on me. I bounced all over the field but managed to get it down. I taxied over to Mr. Canada, and it was the first time I had seen him really mad. He said, "One more of those and you'll go back to Santa Ana." I gulped and started off for the take-off strip again, I managed to do better on the next two landings.

We continued on in flying for four weeks. Our schedule carried ground school in the morning and flying in the afternoon for one week, then flying in the morning and ground school in the afternoon the next. Time seemed to go fast. We thought we were making progress in our flying, and we were becoming used to the hazing. The upperclassmen were good Joes and only doing things that would help us later on, our reason told us. After five weeks I was still in there pitching, but not without times of dejection. The nightmare of all of us was the danger of "washing out."

The upper class was now on their way to Basic and we were to put some dodos fresh from Santa Ana through the paces. The cadets were eagerly awaiting the arrivals from the pre-flight school up the coast. New cadet officers were installed and I was made a flight commander. I was proud as punch of our flight. About thirty-five cadets were in it, and we were determined to be the crack outfit of the school. The new dodos came in and the boys of course hopped on them. I stayed out of it for various reasons, mainly perhaps because I knew the new cadets would especially resent anything from me since I happened to have had a name before entering the service. I could easily see that they would get plenty without my two cents worth, and they did.

The cadets at Oxnard lived in little cabins rather than in tents as at Santa Ana. By the time five weeks had passed we could all have qualified as chambermaids. Our rooms were immaculate. Coming into the upper class made it just as tough on you, because the under class looked to you for an example. Then, too the Tactical Officer of the squadron, Lieutenant Breedon, would make an occasional drive through your rooms, and if he found dust or dirt it meant no pass for the week end. In my cabin were Jerry White and John Bickley. Bick, or "Doc Quack" as we called him, was an old Army man. He knew the

Army like a book and helped us often with suggestions on how to make our life easier. He would often use the old Army man's privilege of griping when things were not as they should be, and that was why we started calling him Doc Quack. In the adjoining cabin were Orv Buckler, John Seymour and Herm Kollmeyer. The six of us formed quite a gang. Buckler and I went all through school together and became fast friends.

One of the features of cadet days is that all roommates worry about each other. Before we finished, two of our six washed out, and we all felt it. Kollmeyer and Buck always had a time with Seymour. Sy was the world's laziest individual but had a heart of gold. Kollmeyer would spend hours fixing his bed and pillow so that he could pass inspection, and then when he wasn't looking Sy would exchange Kollmeyer's beautiful pillow for his messy one. As a result, Kollmeyer would get gigged and Seymour would get the week-end pass. Sy was quite a bit older than the rest of us and knew all the tricks. He had been a traveling salesman in civilian life and considered himself quite the ladies' man. He could always get out of more work than the rest of us could do, and the ways he got out of things always gave us a laugh. We had a good outfit. Everyone rode his forty hour checks and passed, and we felt good.

The time was nearing when we would have to move on to Basic. Things moved fast. The new boys from Santa Ana had come into their own and were a fine class. We had just one worry left, and that was our final check. That ride gave all of us uncertain moments, for it was then that the instructors threw everything in the book at you. Spins, rolls, loops, precision turns. The big day arrived and I went out to perform. I knew I did a lousy job of flying that day, but after a few corrections from my instructor I managed to pass the check.

I was one happy boy that night. Buck, Bickley and Sy got by too. The two of our gang were washed out. We were sorry to see them go, for they were great guys, and friendships that grow out of living and working together are hard bonds to see broken. They both went back to Santa Ana and are now commissioned officers doing a great job. The last I heard, one of them was a bombardier in England and the other a navigator in the Pacific.

We had one final ritual before leaving, and that was a big graduating party. It was a gala affair for all, and closed our careers at Oxnard with a bang. On that night everyone let his spirits soar, and the dance was a huge success. Like everybody else, I had a great time.

The next day we were off to Basic. We had learned how to fly the Army's first plane, and now in a few days we would start to fly the second one. During these days I was ordered back to Santa Ana to appear on a radio program. I flew over and took part in the Army radio show. The audience for the performance was made up of cadets who had not as yet left Santa Ana and of others who had been returned there after a wash-out somewhere along the line. When they saw me on the program back at Santa Ana, right away the rumors started flying. No one stopped to ask why I was back, they just took it for granted that I had washed out too. The newspapers picked up the story, and the rumor really attained proportions. I felt rather hurt about it. I knew too that it would start bad publicity for the Air Forces from some people who would want to know why Tom Harmon was allowed a second chance and wasn't returned as are all the others who wash out. Rumors like that are bad business all around. I wrote a letter to the sports editor of the Santa Ana paper, and he helped me out on it, but the tale couldn't be stopped entirely. I decided the best thing to do was to forget it, but it was to follow me all through my training. About two weeks before I was to get my wings, Jerry White, my former roommate at Oxnard, who was then training as a bombardier, came to the same school where I was training too. Whitey was genuinely amazed to see me still flying, as he had heard I had been impertinent to an officer and had not only been washed out, but that I had been returned to Santa Ana for one day and then sent to Alaska as a private. It made a pretty good story, but I didn't like it much, particularly when I found out that even my former pals had fallen for it. Anyway, in spite of all rumors, I went on flying and loved it.

My class finally arrived at Basic, for which we were ordered to Gardner Field, Taft, California. If I were to pick a favorite school among the ones I hit during training, it would be that one. It wasn't that the school as such was so different, but the officers at Gardner were certainly an outstanding group. The organization couldn't be topped. We ran into the same upper class that we had had at Oxnard, but they were now calmed down and the hazing wasn't half so tough. Flying and schoolwork took up most of their time, so they couldn't bother much about slapping down the underclassmen.

Everyone in our class was amazed at the BT, as the Basic Trainer was affectionately known. It appeared to be full of instruments that none of us would ever be able to master. In comparison with a Primary Trainer, the BT looked like a gadget from Mars. We were organized quickly and went to the flight line to meet our instructors. I was assigned to Captain Bennion, a young Army officer from Salt Lake City and a truly great guy. He had been in the training command for some time and was flight commander. There was nothing about the BT that Bennie didn't know. He ruled the flight with an iron hand, but he was always available if any of the cadets were in trouble. I had a long talk with him before flying and will always be grateful to the good Lord for giving me an instructor like Bennie. As I came to know him he was a lot more than just a great flyer.

In the early stages of flying, a student who is of good size may have the idea that his strength will help him to fly a plane. It is a common misunderstanding, and I was fooled by it too. It didn't take Captain Bennion long to cure me though. During one of our flights, still early in the game, I was clutching that ole stick again with all my might as though my life depended on it. I was so tight that I could have been used as a first class string on anybody's violin. Finally over the interphone came this remark: "Harmon, you big ham, if you don't relax on that stick I'll take the one I have back here out of the socket and bat you on the head with it." It was Captain Bennion speaking, and never after that was I too tense on the controls. Now I had caught on how to be at ease in the BT.

In Basic we started formation flying and instrument work. Formation flying was fun, but the hours spent working on those instruments were dreaded. It takes all sorts of things to make a complete schedule, and though there are many things on it that you do not like, after you get your wings you see that everything all along the line was given you for a reason. It all may come in handy in a pinch.

The Basic Trainer was a larger ship than the Primary Trainer both in size and in horsepower. We had all heard what a killer ship the BT was supposed to be, and it was in Basic that we lost the only member of our class in a training accident. No wonder we were all a little skeptical, but our fears were quickly calmed by Captain Bennion. He told us about the boy who had "spun in" and what had probably happened.

One of Bennie's tricks that put us all at ease was this. "Just remember, boys," he would say, "an airplane is just like a woman. You can't get rough with her, you have to baby her and pet her like a doll, and if you do she'll purr like a kitten. Try throwing her around and she'll bat you down."

We continued our training, and the upper class left for Advanced and our under class came in from Oxnard. We were glad to see them. They had acquired a polish that made them look much different from the bunch of "Ranchy dodos" they were when they had arrived at Oxnard. It had been the same way with us, but we saw it better in the class that came after us than we could in ourselves.

Ground school was getting tougher and tougher, and you began to see that a fellow who managed to get those Silver Wings could honestly claim that he knew how to fly. Gardner was a hard school but a good one. The cadets worked hard all week, knowing that if they did they could be certain of a pass on Saturday. If you got out of line, you still got gigged, and that ramp wasn't worn down just from being looked at. Many a cadet had made a wrong move and had to "walk" it off.

One of my pleasantest associations in Basic was with Major Don Meade, the director of training at Gardner. Major Meade probably had more time in airplanes than our whole class put together. He was like a father to both instructors and cadets. He asked that his cadets meet him halfway in cooperation, but if you did this he never let you down.

One of the instances of Major Meade's backing up his cadets I remember very clearly, for I was involved in it. In one of the nearby counties a Justice of the Peace was getting fat on the traffic fines he collected from the cadets. One Saturday we were on our way to Los Angeles and got caught speeding in his county. Now the cadets had been paying their fines on the line every time they got nailed, for they were afraid that if it was known at school they would immediately get washed out. Whatever exorbitant sum the fines might be, they paid rather than let the field officers know about it. We picked up a ticket this Saturday, and the fine was one hundred and fifty bucks. It was outrageous. That fine meant two months' pay to a cadet, and I just didn't have it. I went to Major Meade, and he straightened out the whole deal. The Justice was forced to lay off his speed trap, and a lot of cadets were saved a whole lot of money. That was only one of the many things Major Don Meade did for the cadets. Another thing he did for them traditionally was to be responsible for a swell graduating party. The boys went out from his school feeling that they had been in contact with a man of real character, and I think his influence on the cadets was quite important.

We graduated from Basic and were at last on our way to the final school, Advanced Flight Training. The boys who had washed out in Basic were few, and the class stuck pretty well together. Buckler, Sevmour, Bickley and I were still together. We teamed up with Paul Waalkes and Moose Koscelnek and once again had quite a gang. Although when the class went on to Advanced it got pretty well broken up, the six of us went on together to Williams Field, Arizona.

We had hoped for twin engine training and were lucky enough to receive our wish. Going to Arizona meant that for the first time since my training began I would be leaving the coast, and I was sorry about that. But it wouldn't be long now if things went right before we had our wings. I only hoped for one thing in Advanced, and that was that I might have an instructor of the same type as Johnny Canada and Captain Bennion. My prayers were answered, for I was placed under Bill Magee. "Maggie," as he was called, was a Second Lieutenant and a thorough pilot. He never missed a trick and devoted his attention to seeing that his students never missed one either. We were now going to fly the Advanced Trainer, the AT-17. It is a two engine Cessna and a swell little ship. It was the first time we had had a chance to handle a two engine job.

Williams is a good school, but it has one fault—it is located on the desert, and we happened to arrive there for the hottest months of the year. It was broiling there, and flying was tough. Maggie gave us formation, cross countries and gunnery. Before we finished we had flown the Army's three best Advanced Trainers, the AT-6, the AT-17, and the AT-9.

On the first of the cross-country flights I started on my epics of getting in Dutch. I was flying co-pilot for a classmate by the name of Bodie Fite who was one of the crackerjack pilots of our flight. He and I were roommates with Waalkes and Brown. The flight we were on was supposed to be very simple. We were just to fly to three towns and return to the field. But for us it turned out to be pretty difficult. Our major checkpoints were mountains, and so far as I had been able to determine from the air, one mountain looks just like another. We probably would have been okay, but there turned out to be a slight error in our compass—something like sixty degrees or so—and we really got lost.

At that point, to make matters rosier, we lost an engine, and there was no choice but to land on the desert. We were somewhere on the Gulf of Mexico, but where exactly—that was the question. The landing was a wheels-up crash job, and Bodie managed it like a charm.

We climbed out of the ship and took a good look around. There wasn't a soul in sight, nor any sign of a town. We did see a road going along by the ocean, but it looked as though it was very little used. We tried to contact the base by radio, but that didn't work and we gave up trying after a while.

We had been sweating things out there on the desert for about two hours when we saw a car coming along the road. "Thank the Lord," I said. We ran over to the road and hailed them. Bodie yelled out, "Where are we, friend?"

A lot of jibber-jabber came back to us in reply. A foreign language! "Ye Gods, we're in Mexico!" said Bodie disgustedly. That just about did for us. We knew now that we were off our course and then some.

The car had stopped, and its swarthy occupants seemed obliging though unintelligible. We used all the inventiveness we could muster on the sign language, and I pulled a few words of college Spanish out of my hat to help things along. Eventually we decided that I would go with the boys in the car, and Bodie would stay and guard the plane. I was taken to a railroad camp about twenty-five miles away, and after quite a parley finally convinced the head man we were Americanos. Once convinced, he helped me in an effort to get hold of the American Consulate on the phone, but it was Saturday and the Consul had gone home, back across the border. We left a messenger trying to track him down, and I went back to join Bodie. Three guards from a Mexican fort that was some distance away came back with me, and after we had cleaned the plane of its valuable equipment we left the Mexican soldiers on guard. We went back to the railroad camp, and the American Consul, who had been located by then, called. We left the next morning by rail for the border.

After traveling all day long, we finally arrived at the Consulate, and the Consul took us over the border in person. You can imagine what our thoughts had been during that long day jogging over the Mexican tracks. We were plenty worried. The Consul had notified the field, and they had said they would fly a couple of planes to an airport nearby and pick us up. We had dinner and a bath at the Consul's home and felt much better but still definitely uneasy. We were too close to getting those wings for the thought of washing out to be anything but torture. We waited around until afternoon, and at last a call came through. The instructors had landed at another field, they couldn't find ours. It cheered us up slightly that we weren't the only ones who could get lost. We drove over to the other field, boarded the planes and were taken back to our own base.

We learned when we got there that people had been really worried about us. Buck, Sy, Waalkes and Moose had all volunteered to give up their day off to search for us—a sacrifice that meant plenty of concern, you can bet. We felt sort of good to think our buddies had been ready to go all out to find us.

We knew we were in for plenty of trouble, though, because Monday morning we had to meet the accident board. A great number of students had been getting lost, but ours was the worst case, so we knew we were in for it. We went before the board, and Bodie got washed out, because he was the pilot of the ship. I was allowed to stay, but was in the doghouse with Maggie, and justly so. I had to watch my step and try my best not to make any more mistakes. I felt it was sort of an injustice for Bodie to have to take it on the chin, but he took it like a man and is now flying for the R.A.F. in England, so he is doing his job and it is a swell one, in spite of his having been denied his Silver Wings.

The time grew near for graduation, and we were working on aerial gunnery. Everyone was all out for it, because it might mean a chance to get a crack at flying the P-38, the plane the majority of us were hoping to draw when we graduated. We had special lectures on the P-38, and a couple of demonstration ships came to the field with their test pilots from Lockheed. These were piggy-back ships with the radio torn out to make room for two to ride in them. The maneuvers that this plane could do on one engine were almost unbelievable. The greatest hope of every one of us was to be assigned to fly this great ship.

Graduation day came, and everyone was as excited as possible. I guess our feeling might be compared to that of a child with a new toy, or maybe it was more like the feeling of a father with a new baby. I wouldn't know, but it was certainly the most special thrill I had ever known. Those Silver Wings made your chest want to stick out a mile.

The majority of the boys had their parents there for graduation. It was a long way to Michigan, and Dad's health had been none too good, so I had told Mom and Dad it would be best for them to stay home. But when the moment came after graduation for someone to pin your wings on, I had no one, and I certainly missed them. It was a wonderful sight, though, to see all those boys with their wives or their mothers pinning those Silver Wings on their chests.

Our orders came out, and the class was split up. Half of the gang were to go to Florida to fly B-26's and the other half to Greenville, South Carolina, to fly B-25's. I was just over the line in the latter half. Buckley, Bickley and Brown were going to Florida, and Waalkes, Sy,

Moose and I were going together to Greenville. I had hoped we could all stay together, but the division was made alphabetically, the first part of the alphabet for Florida and the rest to South Carolina.

The last part of the alphabet was looking forward to flying the B-25. We had felt sure that if our gang could only stick together we could beat the whole Axis all by ourselves, but we still meant to do our darndest. The boys who were going to fly the B-26's got a break at this point. They were given twenty days off, whereas those of us who were to fly the B-25's were to report immediately. I had been hoping to see the folks but now things did not look too well. Waalkes and I were driving my car through, though, so that gave us some travel time. We were bound that we would make Michigan on the way if it was humanly possible.

That was the end of our cadet days. Those days will always remain in my memory. They weren't always carefree, but they were happy and full of good fellowship. The training had been tough and complete, but it wasn't without plenty of fun and laughs. The friendships I had made with my fellow cadets and the fine contacts with my instructors were worth a lot to me. I felt we had been lucky in our instructors; men like John Canada, Captain Bennion and Lieutenant Magee are typical of the men who have trained the pilots of this war. They have a job that isn't easy, a job requiring patience and constant work to achieve perfection. For my money they are champs. I will always remember them and be thankful for their great help. They can play on my beam any day.

Cadet days were over, and from now on, we felt, we would be playing for keeps. Shortly after we arrived at Greenville, the North African campaign started. This was war. We all had the realization that some of us wouldn't be coming back, and it wasn't a happy thought. Like all the boys, though, I felt certain that I would come back. I had faith in the Big Boss upstairs and knew that He was listening to my prayers when I asked Him to watch out for Mom and Dad and give me the strength and protection I would need in order to come back to them. I had the Faith and the confidence to resolve to do all I could to make that dream come true and fulfill my part of the bargain. I didn't have any doubt that the Big Boss was right there on the team—calling signals from the quarterback position.

GREENVILLE AND THE B-25'S

4

IT WAS EARLY IN November that two newly commissioned Lieutenants in the Army Air Forces were driving across the endless plains of Texas. Paul Waalkes and I had become fast friends in our months together as cadets, and we had an extra bond in that we were both from the state of Michigan, and Michiganders are apt to see things in the same light.

We were planning to get in two or three days at home in Michigan before reporting to our new base at Greenville, South Carolina, and by driving night and day we figured we could make it on the travel time we had. We were both pretty proud of our Silver Wings, and looking forward to seeing our homes again before going on, so our spirits were in top condition.

As we were driving along through the desert one day, with me snoozing peacefully while Waalkes took his turn at the wheel, we came to a military reservation. The car came to an abrupt stop, and I was rudely shaken out of my slumber. I looked up out of the window and saw, like a vision, a tall negro soldier standing at strict attention and saluting. Befuddled, I looked around, and so did Paul, to see who the dickens he was saluting. Our car was the only one on the road. Then it suddenly dawned on us. *We* were the guys he was saluting. We were officers now. We lost no time then in returning something really snappy in the line of a salute, and we nearly broke our arms doing it.

We drove straight through to Ann Arbor. I was anxious to see my folks again, and since Paul's fiancée was attending the University of Michigan, he was eager to get to Ann Arbor too. He would have a chance to see her before going on to Grand Rapids for a quick visit with his folks.

It was a proud and happy homecoming for me. I hadn't let Mom and Dad know I was coming, so they had one of the surprises of their life when I walked in late that night. We all just about cried with joy. Mom and Dad, clad in their night clothes, sashayed around getting a snack for Paul and me, their faces beaming as they traveled between refrigerator and table. We sat around talking for about an hour, and all this while Paul was in deep conference on the telephone trying

48

to convince an irate housemother that he simply had to see his girl. It was a matter of Military importance, or so he would have her believe. He finally succeeded in persuading her to grant the interview, and set off for the sorority house to say hello and good-bye. When he returned, we all turned in. A fellow certainly appreciates crawling into his own bed at home after ten months in the Army! I was home and I was happy. I slept the sleep of the dead that night.

It seemed about dawn when Paul and I crawled out again. Mom had golden brown waffles on the table for us, which made up for having to get up so early. Army cooks may, some of them, be fresh from the kitchen at the Waldorf Astoria, but at that, they couldn't hold a candle to Mom's cooking. I took Paul down to the bus station and wished him a pleasant visit with his folks. And now I had the whole day before me, but as yet the day was too young to go and see my old pals.

Never in my life have I been prouder than when I walked down State Street that morning with those shiny Silver Wings. Soon I was back in Slater's Bookstore with all the old gang that was left in town. The main topics that morning were airplanes and the war. Our old heated arguments were as heated as ever, and it was wonderful to be back. I talked my leg off, and if any outsider had been tuned in I am sure he would have thought I had flown every ship the Air Forces ever possessed and one or two others to boot.

Those three days at home made the whole world seem like a rosy bowl of cherries to me, but for Paul the homecoming had been different. He wired me that his Dad had had a stroke. That piece of sad news cast a shadow, but remembering my own concern when I had heard my Dad was sick and in the hospital and I couldn't get home, I was at least glad that Paul was able to be with his Dad. We telegraphed to try to get some extension of our leave and were granted three days. In that time, Paul's Dad rallied to the extent that he was now out of danger, so that Paul could proceed with an easy mind to our new base and new assignment.

I hated to think of leaving home, for it looked as though our chances for another visit with our folks before going overseas weren't too good. We packed our things and started off again, with the hope deep in our hearts that we might get back before we went over.

After driving through the mountains of Kentucky and Tennessee, we came to Greenville. At first sight the little town looked pretty, and the B-25's droning overhead gave notice that we had just about reached our destination. We reported to the field at once and were assigned to quarters. Both Paul and I were assigned to the 371st Bomber Squadron, and later we were thankful for that piece of luck. Our schedule was all cut out for us, and we lost no time setting to work. The field had just received a new contingent of airplanes and needed pilots, so our training with the big ships started at once. We quickly became acquainted around the field and were happy that we had such a great gang of instructor pilots to show us the ropes around the B-25. I was assigned to Lieutenant Bob Wood, a pilot who could make a B-25 sit up and talk. He never exerted himself, he just seemed to let the plane fly itself under his guidance. We had great times when we rode together. Woodsie was a fine singer, and even though I couldn't carry a tune in a basket, you could always hear rousing voices from our plane expounding on the beauties of "Dinah" or some other queen of the popular songs.

After the ships that we had flown in training school, the B-25 was a treat. There was about as much difference between it and a trainer as between an old model T and a new Cadillac. It was a sweet ship, there were great guys in the squadron, and everything went along to match.

Hank Wagner, Smitty, Woodie, Bill Whalen, Moose, Paul and I became quite a gang. The first three were instructors and took the new cubs under their wings for the checks. It seemed like cadet days at first. In the main, though, we felt more than ever that we were members of a great team, a team whose success depended on every man doing his part toward the final goal. It seemed like a big football game, but the goal was life or death. No room for mistakes in this scrimmage.

Our flying progressed rapidly during the months at Greenville. When I first came to the field, I had hoped that somewhere along the line I might be given the chance to transfer to pursuit, and if possible to fly the P-38. I don't know what reason I could give for this desire, I just simply wanted to fly that ship. Many of my classmates felt the same way, I know, for we had many discussions about the greatness of that plane. But now it wasn't the P-38 we were flying, and so I said to myself, "This is war, friend. What do you mean, you don't like the job that you have been given? Well, there are a million other guys in this man's army who may not be quite suited with what they are doing, but they are doing it anyway and a damned good job, too. Don't start asking for favors now, do a good job at what you have been assigned and maybe things will break. Handles!"

It took me just two weeks at Greenville to give up any wish to ask right now for a transfer to fighter type ships. Sure, I still wanted to fly the P-38, but I was happy for the moment flying the B-25. I had come to know her, and that meant to like her. Bombers may come and bombers may go, but I doubt if any other has seen or will see the amount and range of action on all fronts that the "Mitchell" has seen in this war. She was a sweet flying baby and could take it and dish it out with the best of them. And we felt proud that it was our ship that had bombed Tokio.

There was just one thing I remained doubtful about. The first pilot of a B-25 is the commander of the ship, and that means a lot of responsibility. Being in charge it would be my duty not only to pilot the ship, but to see that my crew was protected. This is what I worried about, and yet little did I know at the time how it feels to be responsible when you hit the kind of occasion when all your flying ability, all your training, every trick you ever learned cannot help you out.

The people of Greenville were wonderful. They took great pride in their flyers and treated us like part of the family. They did more in their every-day hospitality and thoughtfulnes, to keep up our morale than did all the Special Service officers in the world. The dances that fall were numerous, and the good-looking girls in town often had trouble deciding which officer to accept as escort for which affair. The flyers were a harmonious bunch at the base and in the air above too, but when it came to dates for the week end, it was a case of dog eat dog and the devil take the hindmost. The holidays were approaching fast, and our amount of flying time was mounting fast too. We would soon be ready to go overseas.

With the coming of the Yuletide, the folks of Greenville grew even more hospitable and kind to the fliers. But Christmas is the special time of the year when every man on earth wants to be home with the ones he loves. On the day before Christmas I was down in the alert shack on the flying line. I was called into our squadron commander's office about another matter, and happened to hear that the squadron needed some papers from Detroit. I asked Captain Willis if I could go on the trip. The Blessed Virgin must have heard my prayers, for I was given the job as co-pilot with Hank Wagner. That meant I would be able to be with my family for Christmas!

Waalkes was to be a co-pilot on the trip too, and we were both happy. I would be with my folks and Paul would be with his girl. We made Detroit in record time, and after clearing up our business we drove out to Ann Arbor. The Harmon clan was there in fine fettle. It seemed like old times. The crew of our plane were bunked all over the house on every available bed or couch, and everybody was happily tumbling over everybody else. Mom Harmon was in her glory.

That Christmas day was one to remember. The Christmas dinner had never tasted better. Presents given and received were exclaimed over, and Sister Mary had her usual little remembrances ready. This year for me it was a fancy road map of Arizona with the boundaries clearly outlined by a large red pencil line, to help me not to stray into Mexico again.

As luck would have it, the weather in Detroit socked in. We couldn't take off as scheduled and were a few days getting back to Greenville. Before the family broke up to go to their homes, we had a long conference of the Harmon kids. I knew that this would be my last chance to see everyone before I went overseas. I cornered Sister Mary after the main talk for a little private conclave. I knew I could count on Mary, in spite of all her joking and cutting up, to keep a clear head through anything. "Look, Sis," I said, "I'll be going across soon. I don't know how long I'll be gone, but I'll be back, I'm sure of that. If ever you hear from the War Department or the newspapers that I am lost, don't let Mom lose faith. I'll be back, sis. Just keep saying those prayers and I'm sure everything will work out."

Later on, I was never more thankful for anything than for having had that heart to heart talk with Mary. Mom didn't need help, exactly, but Mary kept the family keyed up during the dreary days that were to come.

After passing a wonderful holiday with the folks, the crew of our plane returned to Greenville. We really buckled down to work. I had been assigned a crew on a B-25, and we knew that the time couldn't be far off when we would receive those orders to push along. Waalkes and Moose were the two crews ahead of me on the list, so it looked as though we would have a pretty good chance of staying together in combat. The final stages in readying us for the real thing were tough. We had long navigation and overwater navigation flights, gunnery, skip bombing, altitude bombing and night flying. We averaged about eight hours of flying every other day, and that is a long time to be up in the air. The weather in Greenville had turned cold with the coming of January, and the night flying was like being in a refrigerator. We bundled up in heavy winter clothing and still froze on the long hops. The B-25 is a wonderful bomber, but tactical airplanes are not made for all the comforts of home. Their equipment is all there for the sole purpose of seeing that their job is done, and there is nothing about them reminiscent of a big airliner.

Assigned to my crew were a great gang of fellows. Lieutenant Fred Wieting of Lansing, Michigan, was the co-pilot, Lieutenant Ed Wolf from Philadelphia was our navigator, and the enlisted men were Staff Sergeant Goodwin, engineer, Staff Sergeant Coss, radio operator, and Sergeant Len Gunnells as gunner. All the boys were experts in their individual lines. We always clowned around together plenty on the ground, but in the air everything was business.

We made our long overwater hop to Florida, flying off the coast, and had a bit of excitement doing it. The right engine was acting a little troublesome as we were going along the coastline, and after checking it Sergeant Goodwin decided that the best thing to do was to look for a landing field. The engine looked bad and might go completely if we continued our flight. The closest field was at Daytona Beach, Florida. We circled in toward land where the town was supposed to be, but the coast was as dark as the inside of a shoe and the town was completely black.

According to Eddie Wolf, our navigator, the airport was to the west of the town, and since according to his chart we should be exactly over Daytona, we went down. We had complete confidence in Ed's navigation, for he really knew his onions. However, it was more than a bit bewildering not to be able to pick up a single landmark or a bit of light. Daytona had certainly done an outstanding job of blacking out! Lieutenant Wieting kept on trying to contact the Daytona airport by radio, but there was no answer to his calls. We circled down low a couple of times and finally we could make out the town and the runways of the airport. I guess that the tower at Daytona got tired of hearing Lieutenant Wieting call, and when he told them that either they would have to turn on the lights on the runway or else they would have one B-25 splattered all over their town, the lights went on, and we were able to land. It wasn't a bit too soon, for that right engine had been acting worse and worse.

We stayed over a day in Daytona while Sergeant Goodwin fixed up the ship, and then we returned to base. It was only a minor accident on one of our many routine flights, but it showed the fine capabilities of our crew. Every man did his job just right and not one of them showed the slightest nervousness. I was proud of them.

We continued our flights and finally finished all the work scheduled.

The orders for dispatching crews were coming in, but the most recent batch was completed with the crew just before ours. That meant we were separated from Waalkes and Moose. They were sent to the South Pacific, while our destination was to be in the other direction. Then our orders came too and after a final inspection the crews were all set and ready to go. There were three of them from our squadron going over together. I was assigned as flight commander and felt proud of the job. Lieutenant Carter Waugh and Lieutenant Whitey Whitehurst were the pilots of the other two crews.

We were sorry to be saying goodbye to Greenville and its wonderful people, but pilots are always having to push off. We had gotten used to it since we began our training. First Santa Ana, then to Primary at Oxnard, and Basic at Gardner Field in Taft, all three in California. Then Advanced Flight training at Williams Field, Arizona, graduation and getting our Silver Wings, and finally the last stage at Greenville. And the whole thing in about a year! No sooner had you started to know your way around one town than you found yourself starting all over again to get acquainted in some other place. Greenville, like all the other places, had been a swell town to be stationed in, and all of us very sincerely hoped we would be getting back some day to visit our friends and speak our thanks a little better for all the good times they had given us.

If all went according to schedule we should be on our way to a port of embarkation soon. We hoped that we would be picking up new planes at the embarkation point, for the thought of going over the drink in a boat didn't appeal to any of us. We felt confident that we would be able to make the flight across if we were given the opportunity. Ed Wolf was such a crackerjack at navigation that we were sure we could hit all our points and landmarks on the flight.

We were ordered to a port on the Eastern seaboard that was also used to load troops on transports, so we could not be sure that we would get to fly our own planes across. When we arrived at the embarkation base, we found to our delight that we had a nice new B-25 waiting for us. It was a thrilling moment when we first saw our ship. She was all ours, and she was going to be our baby from now on. She was one of the latest models, and even before flying her we could easily see that she was the finest ship in the world. Anybody would have had a hard time to convince her crew that she was anything but perfect.

A delay at the base because of some official papers that didn't come through on time kept us waiting for a while before we could fly down to Florida, where we would take off for overseas. We now had our work laid out for us, though. Each man had a definite job to do, and we had to work a hard schedule to see that everything was shipshape before we took off. We were ordered to remain on call at the post, but that didn't worry the boys too much because they knew we could not take off yet anyway because of some mechanical difficulties with the ship. Once we succeeded in getting a pass to go to town, and our crew went in together. It was quite a party we had that night, and the main subject of our talk was what to name the ship. We finally decided on LITTLE BUTCH. We looked forward to having a painter put her name on, but for the present she was still unchristened.

After a few more days we took off for our first flight. It wasn't a long hop, for we only had to fly to a nearby base to get the remaining part of our overseas supplies. It was a real thrill for us to take the big bomber off the ground for the first time. She was a new ship, and only had a total flying time of about eight hours chalked up for her. She was so new you could smell the fresh paint on the inside of the compartment. We were a proud and happy crew that afternoon when Little Butch took to her wings under our direction.

In two days we had the ship all loaded and ready for overseas. This done, we took off for a routine flight in the local area. On our return we found to our amazement that in doing so we had broken the law of the field. We were greeted with a court-martial on our return! This was quite a surprise, for we had only wanted to find out where our weight was, how it was distributed and how the ship rode with it. It seems that the field wanted no responsibility for crack-ups, and once your wheels left the ground you were not of that field any more. If any accident occurred en route, they didn't have to take the blame. I am sure that this failure to load planes properly was one of the reasons for the Army's loss of planes during the overseas flight. The fault has now been corrected, but it existed at that time. After we had shown that we were only interested in checking up on the safety of the ship and her crew, the charge against us was dismissed.

We had Little Butch ready and were anxious to be on our way. Early the next morning we took off in a jubilant mood. At last we were actually on our way to the last home port. One more stop and we would be on our way overseas.

That night there was nothing in my heart but a sincere desire to get started. Foreign duty was what we had asked for, and now we were actually to get in on the pasting of Hitler and his gang. The tales of

55

combat were flying wide and wicked, but I don't believe even the most hair-raising stories fazed any one in our crew. They were laughing at death or at least they seemed to, and that after all is the only way you can handle this sort of thing.

To me, the crew of Little Butch was the best in the world. I wouldn't have traded any one of them for all the tea in China. We had flown together for quite some time now, and we had the fullest confidence in each other's ability. When the time came for them to show their mettle, I knew they would show it. They would do their darndest to put their training to account.

When we took off the next morning for our last stop in the United States, our crew was happier than ever. The three big B-25's took to the air majestically as big sea gulls. From the time we folded our wheels until we hit Florida, each crew member was working to see how the ship reacted in his special department. Eddie Wolf was checking all the compasses to catch any little error. Sergeant Goodwin was watching the dash panel of the ship's performance as if she was a new baby trying her legs on her first steps. Sergeant Coss was working his radio in communication with the other ships and checking the stations as we went along. The flight overseas wasn't going to be a tea ride. We knew everything had to be right, and responsibility hung heavy on every man's shoulders. The boys were taking no chances they could avoid, and checked and rechecked to eliminate technical failures.

The flight was perfect. Lieutenant Wolf's navigation put us over the field in perfect time. Now we knew for sure that Little Butch was not a slow ship by a long shot. She could move along with the best of them.

We landed and checked in for our final lap. Lieutenant Whitehurst's ship was out for some minor repair, and our time of leaving was delayed for a few days. These days were well spent, though, for we were briefed for the flight and Lieutenant Wolf made certain that every navigational aid was right.

However, the time spent in Florida was a bit restless. The men were supposed to be confined to the field, but once again we knew we couldn't leave on a moment's notice, so the boys had some fun. I was flight commander, so I agreed to stay at the field and be there if any of our gang was wanted for anything. I had a few letters to write, and I knew that Mom would be worried if she knew that we were shoving off. I had heard the boys tell how tough it was to get mail overseas. That is why I had made up my mind that I would write a lot along the way, for, I figured, if all my friends write back, at least some of their replies are bound to get ahead of us to our base on foreign soil, wherever that may be, and will be waiting there for me when we arrive. The letters that night were hard to write, though. The feelings a person gets just before going overseas are mixed. The prospect of adventure gives you quite a thrill, but always in the background there is that cloud of uncertainty. You don't know when you will be getting back, even though you may be sure you will be getting back some time. Now as far as I was concerned, I certainly didn't have the slightest bit of doubt, but getting that faith over to Mom was a different matter. Mothers are always anxious while their boys are away, and I knew mine would worry. I finished the letter, and said a special prayer that the Lord would watch over the crew of Little Butch. Early the next morning I went to the chapel and lit a candle. As I was leaving the church, I stopped in the back and took five medals from the box in the back of the church. I always wore a medal, for Mom had taught me that there is a sure strength gained from this reminder that the Lord is close by. I would never have considered going out on the football field without a medal, and I know wearing it has always helped me.

The crew met at the plane that morning and we had a meeting. We talked everything over and got all set to go. We received word that we would leave the next morning at dawn.

I felt a little funny when, at the end of the meeting, I pulled the five medals out of my pocket. Each had a blue cord on it. I knew that I was the only Catholic among the crew, and I didn't want to hurt any of their private feelings about religion by offering them something of my religion. It was their business. I offered them the medals to take or refuse as they saw fit. Every man of the crew took the little medal and put it on. Days later, it gave me a warm feeling to see, hanging alongside their dogtags, the little medals on their blue cords. I think the boys must have liked them, for they never took them off.

At dawn the next morning we took off as scheduled.

We had our sealed orders and were not to open them until we were on our way. As soon as we were in the air, winging it on our course out over the Atlantic, we opened our envelope.

Our destination was North Africa.

The boys were relieved to know, for the rumors had flown wild and furious about where we would be sent. Into my mind flashed all the stories of Africa I had ever heard. It must be quite a land, but we would see.

Our first objective was Puerto Rico, and before us lay a lot of ocean that I knew must be mighty cold at that time of year. Eddie Wolf was hard at work on his navigation, and Fred Wieting and I were busy flying the ship.

This was it. We were now on foreign service for the United States.

SOUTH AMERICA

5

THE WEATHER FOR THE trip was swell.

We had been briefed that our best altitude would be about nine thousand feet, and that is where we guided the ship. Once we were on course, we took turns flying her. While we were flying in Greenville, we had given every member of the crew some practice in flying the ship, merely as a precaution, so that in case Lieutenant Wieting and I should ever be shot up one of the other boys could take over. Lieutenant Wieting was in charge of the flying right now, and Lieutenant Wolf was working like a beaver among his charts.

After we had been in the air an hour, Lieutenant Wolf told us we were right on course. We had ducked around a few thunderheads, because we were looking for no trouble. After getting past the thunderheads, we put the ship in the hands of "Ole George." That was our nickname for the automatic pilot. On long flights, Ole George can be a God-send. The ship just flies itself by automatically controlled instruments, and all the human pilot has to do is watch.

Puerto Rico was about four and a half hours away, so we settled back and watched George work. We passed over several small islands, and then we recognized the Bahamas as we went over. I remembered having read about the Bahamas in books and newspapers, but I never thought I'd be getting a plane's eye view of the place.

When the time came for our let down, we began to put her to a lower altitude. According to Lieutenant Wolf's calculations we should be over Puerto Rico within half an hour. The weather was clear, and we kept straining our eyes to catch sight of the little island lying in the midst of so much water.

Exactly on the dot, we spotted her right on course. Ed Wolf was on the ball as usual. We called in and circled for our landing. We went in and Lieutenant Whitehurst followed. Then Lieutenant Waugh brought in his ship too. It was about mid-day when we landed at Puerto Rico, and we had taken off from Florida at dawn. We taxied into the line and went at once to see the briefing officer, while Sergeant Goodwin stayed with the plane to give it a check.

At the briefing office we were told that we were to take off the next morning for Port of Spain, Trinidad. It sounded okay, and from the way we were scheduled for the flight we thought they really must want us over there.

Lieutenant Whitehurst came in just then and said that their ship had picked up a leak in the hydraulic line and that they would have to take a day or two on it. Since we were traveling in a flight, we agreed to stick together. About an hour later, Sergeant Goodwin came in to report that Little Butch had sprung the diaphragm on the nose wheel. It wouldn't be any problem to change the part, but since we only had one spare diaphragm we thought we had better send back to Florida for another one. We didn't want to get caught without a spare, and since we were still so near to the States we might as well make good that deficiency.

I had a little doubt whether it was a good move to let our trip be delayed for the sake of a spare part, but we were playing it safe. The delay put us in Puerto Rico for some time, though, and when there is nothing to do time can hang mighty heavy on your hands. We thought we might as well enjoy ourselves while we were there. The field at Puerto Rico is one of our finest bases. They have a bowling alley, a swimming pool, a golf course and a good Officers' Club. We spent most of our time playing cards, the great army pastime. Blackjack and poker and hearts were our games. The boys also took advantage of this interim to write quite a few letters.

We were all of us concerned about Freddy Wieting, our co-pilot. Fred had got married to a swell girl from his home town while he was in flying school. Shortly before Fred left, he had the news that he was going to become a proud papa. His anxiety and concern were shared by the rest of the crew, and we were always kidding him. Fred was a fine boy. He and I had always stuck together, because we were both from Michigan, in spite of the fact that he hailed from the school that was my alma mater's bitterest rival, Michigan State. Fred had volunteered to come along with us as co-pilot, but we knew he wouldn't be with us long after we reached combat, for he was too good a pilot to be riding as co-pilot. Fred was the next to youngest on the crew and the only one of us who was married. He used to talk to us like a father when he was kidding along, he being the only man among us with any experience of the world. Or so he claimed.

The crew of the Little Butch didn't seem like a fighting crew to an outsider. The boys seemed like brothers, clowning around a lot, and if they had a serious thought in their heads, doing their darndest to keep it quiet. There were three officers and three enlisted men, but nobody ever thought of rank. We had perfect cooperation between us. Just asking for help on a particular job was all that was needed. The boys understood each other, they worked as a team and knew it was all for the benefit of Little Butch and her crew as a whole. Thinking of them always reminds me of those posters that used to be around picturing the teamwork of a bomber crew, for as I look back on it now I can see that the gang flying the Little Butch could have been the personification of perfect synchronization. I guess it must be about the same with every crew and their ship. No matter what ship you fly or who the guys in the crew are, you are convinced that your ship and your crew are the best on wings. You may start out inwardly admiring some other type of ship, but after a while you get so sold on the one you are flying that you soon get convinced there is nothing to beat it. If a flier hasn't confidence in his ship, in himself, and in his brother crew members, he can't be worth much. But nothing of the sort could ever be said about any of our crew. We had real confidence in each other. We knew that if the crew of Little Butch got the chance, they would do more than their share in showing Adolf and his supermen what it was like to be really socked.

The spare part that we were waiting for finally arrived. Sergeant Goodwin got right on the job and we were soon ready to go. The afternoon that the plane was ready, Lieutenant Wieting, Sergeant Goodwin and I took her up for a test hop. We thought she was a little tail-heavy the way she was loaded, so we decided to take everything out and do the job over again. It meant a lot of work, but every member of the crew pitched in and by ten p.m. that night we had everything all set. The next morning we took her up for another short hop, and things were perfect.

The next day at dawn we said good-bye to Puerto Rico. Once again

The crew of the first Little Butch before take-off at Puerto Rico. (L. to r.) Wolf, Goodwin, Harmon, Gunnells, Wieting, Coss.

our view was of miles and miles of ocean. After a conference among the crew, we had decided on following the islands down to Trinidad. It would make it a little longer flight, but if anything of a serious nature were to go wrong we would have a chance of making one of the small islands. We were taking no chances on going into that ocean. The flight was a little more exciting this lap, for we ran into a little weather about two hours out of Puerto Rico. Little Butch rode the updrafts like a bird and we came into Trinidad. Once again Eddie Wolf's navigation had been on the button. Due to the bad spot of weather, we had lost Lieutenant Whitehurst, but his plane followed us right in.

Trinidad was quite a spot. The name was familiar to everyone and we were all curious to see the town. Our flight the next day was to be a short one, only as far as Georgetown, so we decided we could go into Trinidad and look things over. This was the first chance we had had to see what a foreign town was. It may have been picturesque, but it wasn't long before we knew that even the worst slum district in the States was heaven by comparison. We began to realize, if we didn't before, how lucky we were to be Americans.

As we got farther away from home, the everyday comforts we had always taken for granted began to drop off. Warm showers ended at Puerto Rico. At Trinidad they were cold. The Post Exchanges along the way got worse and worse. Whatever you asked for, you could be sure they didn't have any of that. What they did have you somehow never wanted. It was beginning to look like war.

Lieutenant Wolf, Lieutenant Wieting and I went into town. We decided to go to the country club for dinner, as it was supposed to be the best place in town. They told us we could get a cooling drink there, too.

Well, any resemblance between what we got and a cooling drink was in name only. I felt I hadn't been away from the States long enough to be able to drink that stuff, the Trinidaddies could have it. For the time being, until I got considerably thirstier, I would get along without their "cooling drinks."

They had a dance that night at the club. We didn't have dates, of course, and cutting was frowned upon. The club was mostly filled with officers of the British Navy. We were pretty tired, so we didn't mind too much just watching the others dance. It brought back memories of home. As we watched the couples glide by, I wondered, "How long will it be till I get back home to a dance?"

We had only a two hour flight before us the next day, so we took off at about ten o'clock. We had been right on schedule since leaving Puerto Rico. Flights were always scheduled with a take-off early in the morning, or if it was a short flight at least early enough to get over the weather before it built up too much. The Army was having us follow the safest course.

We had a little more excitement on the trip to Georgetown. Little Butch was acting up. When we were about thirty minutes out of Georgetown we blew a hydraulic line. The fluid shot all over Lieutenant Wieting in the co-pilot's seat, and you could have heard him holler over on the mainland because it ruined his last clean pair of pants. We laughed at that moment, but it was no laughing matter. No hydraulic fluid meant no brakes, and the B-25 wasn't the type of ship to land without brakes. When she came in, she came in fast; and we had to keep our airspeed in flight because we were so heavily loaded. Sergeant Goodwin found the leak and patched it up as best he could while we were in the air. We called the control tower at our destination and notified them of our trouble. It was no picnic before landing, wondering if we still had any brakes or not, but the Lord was with us. There was apparently enough fluid left in the system to give us enough brakes to get in.

We informed engineering on the field that we were out of hydraulic fluid and in need of repairs and a new hydraulic gauge. They just laughed at us. "This is South America, chum, parts are just things that we read about down here."

The fluid had soaked Lieutenant Wolf's parachute and also Sergeant Goodwin's. They had their 'chutes under the pilot's compartment, as they always did when we were flying. I told them they had better take them over and have them repacked, as we would be staying over a day. The Commanding Officer of the post had different ideas, though. We were informed that night that we would leave the next morning before daybreak. It was another case of rushing, we felt, but we could do nothing about orders.

We were hustled out of bed at three bells and had breakfast so we could get a five o'clock start. We had been briefed the night before and we knew that this was the toughest part of the trip. It was in this stretch that the worst weather would be waiting for us. It never got good, we had been told, and the best you could hope was to fly over it, but most of the time you had to bust through it on instruments.

They had fixed the leak in the line, but the gauge was still out. It wasn't important enough to worry about, at least not in comparison with that weather we had to bat through.

The flight was perfect that morning. We took off at dawn. The sun busted over the horizon and everyone was happy and jubilant. Eddie Wolf had us right on the beam with navigation, and we couldn't see any weather ahead as far as we could look. There was no sign of all that stuff we had been told about. The clouds had only just started to build up.

But they built up fast. We had been briefed the night before that we could get over them at 9,000 feet, but that advice had been on the screwy side, for we were now flying at 11,000 feet and the clouds were still some eight or nine thousand feet above us. It would be about another hour before we would be running into the bad weather, so we were not letting it worry us too much as yet. We were all set for come what might.

About ten minutes before we hit the clouds I called Lieutenant Whitehurst and told him to take a forty-five degree course for three minutes and then pick up his heading so we wouldn't be bumping heads in that soup ahead of us. Whitey picked up his heading, and into the clouds we went.

I had seen some bad weather in my time, but nothing to compare to the stuff we were going into now. If Little Butch had been stripped down, we might have been able to get over it, but not the way we were loaded. So we waded in.

We were tossed around in the thunderheads like a feather. It was as if we had entered a pitch black room. Rain fell by the bucket instead of by the drop. It beat hard against the ship. We had to turn on the fluorescent lights in order to see our instruments. We were fighting to keep Little Butch on course. Both Lieutenant Wieting and I were at the controls to steady the ship. We would lose or gain a thousand feet of altitude as though it were nothing, and it happened so fast you felt as if you were riding in an elevator suddenly gone mad.

After about an hour of this kind of instrument work we felt we were getting hardened to it. We belted along talking about anything and everything. After another fifteen minutes or so we came to an open spot. It was quite a large hole and gave Lieutenant Wolf a chance to see the ground. He caught his bearings at once, for directly under us was the famous French penal colony of Devil's Island. We were right on course.

After a while Lieutenants Wolf and Wieting and I went into a huddle and decided we would try to get under the stuff. It was too violent in the clouds. From where we were, at about 10,000 feet, it looked as though we might be able to break under it. Our course had now taken us inland a bit, but this part of South America is comparatively flat, so there was no danger of our hitting a mountain. We cut back the throttles and started a slow spiral down.

We had finished about two complete 360 degree turns when all hell broke loose. It sounded as though a cannon had gone off. Lieutenant Wieting yelled: "The wing! It's tearing off!" I tried desperately to right the ship, but there wasn't much I could do. "Here we go!" I thought. I wasn't scared, I just accepted it like that. "Here we go!" Then I knew that this was the end of Little Butch and that I must give the order: "Bail out!" And so I did.

The ship went into a sharp spiral to the right. That wing wasn't doing us a bit of good. We were losing altitude fast when Lieutenant Wieting left his seat and went out the bottom escape hatch. We were now at about 4,000 feet and going down like a piece of lead. I looked behind me and could see no evidence of anyone in the ship. I ripped open the top escape hatch, and the ship snapped into a dizzy spin to the left.

She was winding up at great speed now. There was nothing to do but get out. With the tearing off of the right wing, the right motor began to cut out too. Little Butch couldn't ever come out of that spiral. I had to move fast to get out, I had waited pretty long. I reached for the top hatch.

In starting to get out of the ship, I was caught by the terrific pressure of the slipstream. I put my foot on the throttle quadrant and forced every ounce of strength into my football legs. I bolted out of that ship. Knowing I must be near the ground, I reached at once for the ripcord, but missed. On the second try I got hold of it and it must have worked. I had snapped out, and I had no consciousness of the chute having opened. When I came to and opened my eyes I was bouncing in the top of a tree. The chute had been caught in the branches before there had been time enough for it to open fully.

The sight that met my eyes was not a pleasant one. Almost directly below, not more than twenty feet away, were the fiery remains of our once proud Little Butch. I was shaking like a leaf, and I felt that I had truly been watched over, it was that close to the end. The guns in the ship were loaded, and at this point they started to go off in the raging fire. I could hear the shots and could see the bullets going all over the place.

It was raining like hell. I was soaking wet. I was shaking so that I could hardly get my breath. I was afraid one of those bullets might come my way. I didn't dare to move because I didn't know how well that chute was hooked up in the branches above me.

After a moment I calmed down a bit and started to swing in my chute towards the trunk of the tree. I was about forty feet from the ground, and a fall from there would probably mean a broken leg, but I had to take the chance. Little by little my momentum picked up, and I finally swung far enough to be able to grab a limb of the tree. I pulled myself over to the trunk and unbuckled the chute while I held onto the tree with my legs. Then I hung onto the chute long enough to take the things out of my jungle kit which was strapped to the back of it. The compass, bolo knife, chocolate bar, quinine, matches, mosquito netting, and iodine were like a gift from above, and as I looked at them I was more than thankful that I had packed that kit. I put everything I could in my pockets and slipped down the trunk of the tree. When I hit solid ground I was trembling like a leaf again. I fell to my knees and said three Hail Mary's in thanks for having been helped out of that one.

When I tried to get back to my feet, I felt a sharp pain in my right foot. Looking down, I saw that I had torn off the sole of my shoe somehow. It was a clean job, the sole torn off as if a shoemaker had used a sharp knife on it.

The plane was burning heavily, and bullets were still going off. I ducked behind a large tree trunk and waited there until the ammunition had all exploded. I couldn't get near the ship-as yet because of the intense heat, so I started to search the immediate vicinity of the wreck, calling out at the top of my lungs as I did so. I hoped one or more of the boys might have landed nearby and would hear me. It was useless. The noise of the rain in the heavy jungle foliage drowned out my voice. I came back to the ship and waited. Eventually the fire abated a little. I could now get near enough to start investigating.

The tail assembly was about all that was left of Little Butch. Her side was split open. I looked in. There was somebody still in there. He was dead. I could make out that it was Sergeant Gunnells. The shock hit me right in the pit of the stomach. Then I managed to go on checking all around the ship. I didn't find anything else there. But a short distance away from the front of the ship I saw an arm that had been torn off at the shoulder. There was a propeller tattooed on it, so I knew it was Sergeant Goodwin's left arm.—That meant at least two of the boys had been killed in the crash. The blow was all the worse because up to that point I had taken it on faith that the rest of the boys had got out too. And now Goodie and Gunny had flown their last flight.

I stumbled back to the tree where I had pulled some things from the fire and sat down in the pouring rain. I couldn't think of anything but the boys, and how happy we had been before we took off. Where were they when I turned around for a last look before bailing out? I had seen no one. I surely should have seen Goodwin, because his regular position in the plane was only a few feet away from the pilot's compartment. He must have been under the compartment trying to get his chute. I just couldn't figure it out.

I felt like hell itself, but I had to get out of this jungle and could not afford to waste time. The rest of the boys must be wandering around somewhere, and it was up to me to get out and get a search party to hunt for them.

I got down on my knees again and prayed a long prayer. Then I started searching for things that would help me in getting out of the jungle. There was the life raft. It had been thrown free from the ship and contained about six cans of purified water. The cans had been crushed a little, but when I shook them I could hear water inside. I fashioned a knapsack out of a pair of pants by tying the legs together with one end of a rope and the top with the other. In it I placed all the cans of water. I also took a couple of pairs of shorts and two clean undershirts that had escaped the crash. I must have been in some haze to bother about those things. The constant rain kept them soaking wet and they were never any earthly good to me. I found a bailing bucket that had been thrown out of the raft and I took it along to catch the rain as it fell from the sky in case I should run out of water. I was dressed in a flying jumper that had the sleeves cut off above the elbow and as I knew that this would be little protection against the cold, I put on one of the heavy jackets that had been thrown free of the plane. Later on I was very thankful for this move. The jacket not only protected my arms against the mosquitoes but also gave me some protection during the cold, drizzling nights. It was always soaking wet, but still it kept in the heat from my body. Finally I managed to salvage another pair of shoes. I put them on and threw the old ones away. I don't know what would have happened to my right foot in the jungle if I had tried to get through with no sole to my right shoe.

I hunted in vain for a map among the wreckage. I had some idea where I was, from our last bearings before the crash, but at best I could only make a guess. Rather than take a chance and shoot for the closest way out, I took a stubborn resolve to go due east. I knew that in that direction must lie the ocean, and if I could only hit the coastline I would have the best possible chance to get back to civilization. Also, I knew that planes took the coastal route, and therefore I might have some chance of attracting attention. If not, well there were sure to be towns along the coast.

I knew nothing at all about what existed inland in this vast area, except what I saw around me. I put the mosquito net over my head, held the compass in my left hand, the bolo knife in my right, and started off. My knapsack was slung over my shoulder.

My first idea was to try to get to a mountain or to a hill and see if the coast was visible. I felt sure it couldn't be too far away, perhaps fifty or sixty miles. I walked through the jungle for about half an hour before it was borne in upon me that I would see the coast only when I stumbled into the water. The jungle was so dense that my vision was limited to about ten or twenty yards. Most of the time I could only see small spots of sky through the thick foliage, so closed in was that dense roof of leaves. There could be no such thing as a real lookout point.

For hours on end I went along hacking my way through brush and vines, always referring to the compass in my left hand. I crossed two small mountains and came to my first swamp. I took one look at it and wanted to make a detour. It was made of brown and black muck, with buried trees, and vines reaching their tangled tentacles across everything. But I had said I would go east come hell or high water, and so I plowed in.

The first step in that black slush felt as weird and uncanny as anything I have ever imagined. I could feel the black mud go into my shoes and around my legs. Tangled vines caught me and I had to work them loose. By zigzagging along the tree trunks that were under water, I managed to have a pretty fair footing. Often I would slip on the treacherous roots, though, and slide down helplessly. Every time this happened it felt like a blunt razor mowing my skin; I usually slid down scraping my leg from ankle to knee before I could grasp something to save myself. All the while I carried my compass in my mouth. I just had to keep it safe, that was all there was to it.

Finally I saw land about ten yards away and could stick straighter to my east heading. What a feeling of relief to hit solid ground again! Now there was another little mountain ahead of me. I could not see it but I could tell because my footing was on an upward slope. Constant rain had made the red clay underfoot as slippery as a banana peel. Only by grabbing some little bush and pulling myself upwards, or by using the knife as a handle in the ground, could I go up the mountain side, which kept getting steeper and steeper.

I prayed that I would be able to keep up my strength, and I thanked the good Lord for having given me a pair of football legs. According to my watch it was five-thirty in the evening, but even without it I would have known that night was coming on, for the darkness in the sky was fast gathering. I had crossed three little mountains and three swamps that first day. I figured roughly that I must have traveled about fifteen miles in all but that probably meant no more than three miles in the direction in which I had to make progress.

I started up the fourth little mountain. The hills in this region were about seven hundred to a thousand feet high. I decided that I would try to make my bed each evening on the top of a mountain, for I had heard that there are not so many mosquitoes on higher ground. The idea was sound enough, but the hills didn't prove to be quite high enough. The little pests were everywhere. When I had reached the top of this hill, I picked out a large tree trunk that was three-fourths hollow and built a little lean-to for protection from the rain. I had picked up this trick when I was a kid, and it proved pretty useful. There were large palm leaves on some of the trees, and I used these over a framework of branches as a sort of roof. It helped a little in that it kept some of the rain out, but that feature seemed to appeal just as much to the mosquitoes as it did to me.

I had not felt hungry all day, but my mouth was very dry. I had decided that I would not drink unless I absolutely had to. That seemed to be now. I took my little knapsack off my shoulder and first took out the chocolate bar. One small nibble of it only increased my thirst, so I put it away again. I grabbed one of the cans of water and pried off the top. When I tried to drink, only a few drops of water trickled out. The can had run dry in the knapsack.

I took out one can after another, only to find them all the same. The crash had loosened the caps enough so that all that precious water had leaked out.

Now I got filled with a blind fury. All the time I had been plowing through those swamps or crawling across a mountain I had had the comforting thought that I had water. I had kept myself from drinking any of it in order to save it for the time of greatest need. Now it was gone.

The few drops of water left in the cans helped me a little, but I wanted to drink and drink. My head cleared and I realized that I had to muster all the patience I could in order to beat this thing. Losing my head would only defeat me. I crawled into my little hut and settled down for the night.

I quickly found that mosquitoes don't seem to need any sleep. I had the net over my head, but it didn't cover my wrists and ankles, and those mean little single engine jungle dive bombers had found the range in less than no time. They also managed to land on my face, for the net fell flat against my skin when I lay down. It was impossible to sleep. If they weren't biting me, they were soaring around my ears sounding as loud as the motors of a B-17 in the deserted jungle. Aside from the buzz of the mosquitoes, there was only the steady drip-drip of the raindrops on the palm leaves to beat a sickening melody. I felt desperate.

I made a little cross of twig and put it inside the net on top of my head. This kept the net from falling flat against my face, and momentarily stopped my tormentors. I rolled myself into as small a ball as possible and fell into a deep sleep of exhaustion, saying Hail Mary's as fast as I could as I dropped off. The sleep was short-lived, however. I found that it was only possible to sleep in snatches. A large raindrop would hit me in the eye or a twig would bounce off the netting, and I would awaken with a start. I slept with the knife stuck in the ground about a foot from my right arm. It was the only means of protection I had, although against a wildcat it would have been very little use. I was bound and determined that any wild animal that attacked me would have one hell of a fight before he got me. The day we left Georgetown, Sergeant Gunnels had taken my gun to clean it while we were on the trip. It was the first time I had flown without it strapped at my side. So the knife was my only weapon.

After awakening about ten times during the night, the luminous dial of my watch told me it was about time for dawn. The sky began to get light. At about five-thirty I hit the trail again.

I knew it was an awful lot to expect, but every morning before starting out I said a prayer to the Blessed Virgin that today might be the day I would hit the ocean. Day after day I failed to reach it, but I never gave up hope.

The second day was once again filled with swamps and little mountains. I held to my direct heading of east and belted on. Occasionally I would cry out as loud as I could. I suppose my voice might have carried as far as a hundred yards, but not much farther, for the constant patter of rain seemed to drown out all sounds except the unusual calls of the jungle birds. It was on this second day when I was tramping and slipping through a swamp that I suddenly heard a cry like the howl of a dog. My heart jumped with hope. I yelled as loud as I could. "Hey, there! Hello!" Where there was a dog there should be a man. But my yells got lost in the sodden noise of rain falling, and I didn't hear the sound like a dog-howl again. It must have been one of those weird jungle birds, or perhaps some wild animal.

From this time on I started saying Hail Mary's as loud as I could. Saying them gave me the comfort of prayer and it might also notify anybody who heard my loud beller that a stranger was wandering in the vicinity. I knew there were head-hunters in this area, but I didn't care—any human being would be a welcome sight. I don't know what made me think that a head-hunter would have come to find me if he had heard me bellowing out a Hail Mary, more than likely he would have been scared away. However that may be, so far I had come upon no traces of human beings. Nobody seemed ever to have been in this jungle.

The day went on. I had cut through five more swamps and had crossed six more mountains. My strength was still with me, but I didn't know how long it would last. I didn't feel hungry, but I thought I had better eat something in order to keep my strength up. The evening before I had put a chocolate bar in the knee pocket of my flying suit. I couldn't have thought of a worse place for it, I discovered, for when I reached for it that night, it was nothing but slush. I had not reckoned with the swamp mud and all that goes with it. The chocolate had got mixed up with plenty of slush, and was mostly muck and maggots now. I threw the stuff away, although that meant I had no food at all and would have none unless I found something on the trail. So far the jungle had yielded nothing but rain. I had seen some berries, but I didn't know what they were and didn't dare eat them.

I still felt confident that I would get out of the jungle somehow if my strength stayed with me. The food situation didn't seem to bother me, but I thought the lack of water would kill me soon. I kept walking along doggedly, but my mouth felt as if it was full of dry wads of cotton. I couldn't get enough saliva to spit. My lips had begun to crack.

I started up another small mountain. The jungle heat was steamy and humid, and I was sweating profusely. I would have liked to throw away my heavy flying jacket, but it was a life saver at night in the cold, so I kept it. Still near the base of this mountain, I stumbled into a small stream. I knew I would be a goner if I didn't get a drink soon, but the water was filthy and I could not drink it. I followed the stream up the mountain. At the top the water flowed over some white rocks. It was near its source and looked clear and clean here. I took a handful and drank. Never in my life had anything tasted so good. I took two more handfuls and drank them slowly. Then I bent and dipped my hot face in the stream gratefully, but I didn't drink any more. I would have liked to drink the stream dry, but I knew a bloated belly would do me no good, so I held back.

So far I thought I had heard airplanes far off twice, and I felt sure that there must be planes out searching for us. In my knapsack I had a rocket pistol and three cartridges which had been thrown clear of the wreck along with the life raft, and I thought if I could use the flares as a signal I might be able to attract attention to my position. However, I could tell that the planes I had heard were some distance away, in the direction I was going in. I thought the sound was closer the second time, and hoped that meant I was headed in the right direction to reach the coast. I was saving my flares to use at the right moment.

The rain continued intermittently, that is, it would rain for three hours then there would be a fifteen minute intermission before it started again. Occasionally the sun busted through a hole in the clouds. Every time it did, I swung into action to check my compass by the sun. With the help of my accurate watch I was able to make what seemed to me a reliable check, and my faith in my little compass was thereby sustained. It was quite a comfort to be absolutely certain of my direction.

I didn't know if the flare pistol would work, and I was anxious for the moment to try it. Once when I had heard the drone of plane motors I tried to start a fire. But that was impossible, for the jungle was so wet, nothing would burn.

I spent the night on top of a little mountain again. The mosquitoes were still with me, and I had reconciled myself to the idea that I was bound to get malaria, but I would certainly get back to civilization first! I didn't want to get any sickening fever while I was still plowing through the jungle. The bites themselves no longer tormented me as they had at first. I was all chewed up and was beginning to get used to it.

At dawn on the third day I was again on the trail. It was five-thirty, for I tried to stick to the same schedule as far as I could. The day seemed even hotter and stickier than the last. I was rambling eastward through the jungle and yelling out my Hail Mary's when I came to a good sized stream at the bottom of one of the mountains. The stream whirled and went off in a northerly direction. I had often heard that it is a good idea to follow a stream, because it leads you to low land, and in any other situation I might have done so, but not in this jungle. I had walked through too many swamps to want to see any more low land than I had to.

I found a log across a small stream and walked out and sat on it. I took my bailing bucket and pulled bucket after bucket of water from the stream, pouring the cool stuff over me—clothes and all. It cooled my heated body and gave me new energy. That bailing bucket had come in pretty handy, although not in the way I had figured on when I took it as part of my equipment.

The drink I had taken from the stream at the top of the mountain had given me a strong temptation to follow every small stream I came to, but I didn't do it. I knew time was an important factor, and that was what I was working against. My strength could only last about so long, and there was no use frittering it away following little streams.

Again that morning I heard the sound of planes, but I could see nothing. It was not yet the right time to use my flares. I hoped that they would still work when the time came, and not have disintegrated in the swamp like my chocolate bar. When I raised that pistol in the air and shot, I wanted it really to have a chance of being seen.

After getting well cooled off in my self-made shower, I continued on my way east. I crossed a few more swamps and a few more mountains. I was going down a mountain yelling my lungs out when suddenly a sight ahead of me made my heart bound. It was blue sky and white clouds, and a lot of them! It meant the jungle had opened up.

Had I reached the ocean at last? I started on a dead run toward the light and clearness ahead. Panting, I reached the spot and pushed away the brush and vines. I saw a large swamp before me in the open.

73

The swamp grass stood about a foot above the water, and from a plane it probably looked like a grassy knoll. Beyond the swamp I could see more mountains. It was the first time I had been able to get any sort of view of the country through which I was passing. This opening seemed like a direct pat on the back to my confidence. It gave me a feeling of being in the open again, out under the sky instead of being choked up in the suffocating jungle with no vision except for a few feet around and above you. Suddenly coming out into the clear air of heaven again, you realize what wonderful things sky and air are. It was like a revelation.

I was more than ever determined that I would push on and that I would get back. I knew there was still a long way to go, and that there was more jungle on the other side of the swamp, but for the time being anyway I would be out where I could see the sky and see any planes that might go by. The rain had stopped, and I felt good. I was glad that the Big Boss upstairs hadn't called my number yet, I loved life and wanted to get home again. I wanted to get happily married and live in a house and raise a family. I thought of my sweetheart and of Mom and Dad, and I remembered my words to Mary before I left home: "Look, Sis, remember that regardless of what the newspapers or anybody else may say, I *will* be back." And I would. It was my duty, not just for myself. The important thing was that some of the boys were still somewhere in that hellhole too, and maybe they had been injured in their jumps or something and couldn't travel. I had to get out and get help back to them.

I stood and thought of the folks and looked at that swamp. I thought of Butch and looked at the swamp again. It was a big thing, it must have been three miles or so across, and in the middle there was a little island. The time was now about late noon, and I decided to make for the little island to spend the night. I knew that those little mosquito bombers would be thicker than blackberries out there, but I also knew that I couldn't make the whole swamp before dark. I certainly didn't want to get caught wandering around in a swamp in the pitch dark. It was tough enough to do in the daytime.

I started into the swamp, and when my feet hit the water I shivered. It felt like going in swimming with your clothes on after you had stayed out on the beach to get dry. The water was cold, and the swamp grass made the going tough. I had not been in the swamp very long before I was aware of a sting on my face. The swamp grass cut like a razor blade. I was too busy trying to keep hold of the compass in my

74

mouth and the bolo knife in my right hand to do anything about it. The stiff, sharp grass kept beating into my face, and the cuts hurt like blazes, but I had my course set for that island and I was going to get there. The water came up to my chin. I was just tall enough to have a footing on the mucky bottom and keep my chin above water. I was about halfway to the little island when I heard a drone in the sky above me. It was a C-47 Army plane, and was coming right over me at only about 400 feet altitude. I struggled to get at my knapsack, but it was no use. The ship went right over my head while I was struggling in the swamp grass. I hoped against hope they might have seen me, but I knew they couldn't have. The plane flew on, probably back to its base.

It took me about three hours more to make the island. For the first time, I took off my clothes and hung them on a tree to dry. The sun was out and the rain seemed to have gone away for the time being. I took everything off except my shoes. I knew that my feet were swollen from going over all that tough terrain and that my right foot especially would be sure to expand all over the place if I ever took off my shoes. That right foot of mine had taken quite a shock when I had parachuted down through the jungle trees and the sole of my old shoe had been torn away. So now my shoes had to stay on no matter how much I would have liked to take them off.

I noticed a couple of hornets, and knew that the island must have quite a colony of them. I went cautiously, for I didn't want them to take a dislike to me. When night approached, I started to build my little shelter, and it was then that I made a bad move. I reached up to one of the palm trees to grab a leaf, and whizz! the hornets attacked. Their nest must have been in that tree. The attack was swift and sudden, and so was my retreat. I tore around that island at a speed that would make Whirlaway look slow, with the hornets in hot pursuit. After a few minutes, though, they lost interest and quieted down, and I managed to get in a pretty good night's sleep. I was awakened at about four o'clock by the rain, and had to put on my heavy jacket again. My clothes were wet once more, but that didn't make any difference, for I had the other half of the swamp ahead of me anyway.

Surveying the swamp before plunging in, I could see some clear spots of water with no grass. That meant deep water. I decided that my best bet was to cross in the direction that seemed to have grass showing on most of it, for if I did go down I could always pull myself up by the grass. I started in, and after about an hour had gone about

300 yards. The grass thinned out there. So I worked my way to a small soddy spot and stepped off. The water was quite deep and vines tangling around my feet made swimming impossible. I went down, swallowing a large amount of swamp water. I fought my way up for breath and then went down again. I thought that the end had really come. I hit the bottom again, braced my legs on bottom and gave a big push. I shot up again, grabbed a big breath, and again went down. This time I tore off the heavy jacket and my knapsack. Shedding this weight was a great help, for the sheepskin-lined jacket weighed a ton when it was wet. I had a hard time getting a breath of air and still keeping the compass in my mouth without taking in all the swamp water in the area and swallowing the compass to boot. Swimming was impossible, but pulling myself out was also impossible since there were no weeds that weren't under water. I started to get panicky but a quick word to the Blessed Virgin cleared the ole head again. My only out was to keep on doing exactly what I had been doing. Hit bottom, bounce up for a breath, go down again, up again, down again. . . . This was about the only solution. I gained about two yards a bounce in this fashion.

When I was up I could see that there was a grassy spot about forty yards away. So I set out to reach it. I had just about made it when I felt sure my lungs would burst. Under water and near the grass was a soft patch of weed that was only about a foot down. I grabbed it with my left hand and pulled myself up on top of it. By lying flat I could stay on top of the water. I was exhausted, and took deep breaths as I lay there relaxing. I stayed in that position about fifteen minutes getting my breath and then started out for the grass and made it.

I had lost the pistol and flares now, as well as my protection against the cold nights. I don't know which I minded losing the most, the flares which meant hope of rescue or the jacket which meant a little immediate comfort. I still had the bolo knife and the compass, though, and so long as I had them all was not lost.

Without my jacket, the swamp grass cut my bare arms like whips. The feeling was sort of like when you draw your tongue over the edge of a paper envelope, and the cuts were like paper cuts, stinging and small. I managed to stay near the grass for the rest of the trip across the swamp.

At last I hit land. I dragged myself up onto solid ground and lay still for about half an hour. The swamp had taken just about all I had.

After my rest, I started out again. I was still heading due east. I came to the top of a small mountain and started to build my little shelter. It was driving cold and I got the chills. I lay down to sleep and dropped off, but woke up after about an hour shaking with cold. The mosquitoes were driving in worse than ever on my unprotected arms, but my body was so exhausted that I fell into another short nap soon.

The fifth day seemed like the worst of all. It was raining hard and the mosquitoes were vicious. I battered my way along, going through two or three more small swamps and over a couple of mountains. At about two o'clock in the afternoon I came to another opening. Since I had had nothing to eat and very little to drink, I was beginning to feel conscious of my strength waning. I came to this new opening with a mixture of hope and apprehension. It was another large swamp.

I just didn't have it. I fell to my knees and prayed for all the strength I could muster. I was worried about Mom. By now she must have got that telegram from the War Department. I had to get out, I just had to get out.

Settling down to business once more I decided for the first time to change my course. I couldn't hold to my due east heading because I knew I could never make it through that swamp. I had crossed one and I knew. I decided to pick up a northeast heading and go around the swamp in that direction. I guess the Lord must have been watching out for me when I made that decision. It was what was finally to get me out.

I started around the swamp. I must have gone about three miles when I came upon a sight that stopped me in wonder. There was a green bottle and some broken green glass lying beside the swamp! I could hardly believe my eyes. I just stopped and stared, and said a silent prayer of thanks. Then I started searching around feverishly, and found several more bottles. I put them in a line and looked at them. It meant there must have been somebody around here in this God-forsaken place, maybe there was somebody close at hand. My hopes soared.

I kept on circling the swamp, and soon I spotted a tree that bore a small but definite blaze. Somebody had cut that tree with a knife. I prayed that the mark wasn't made by some poor pilot lost like me, that it was really a sign of civilization. I knew though that several boys had gone down in this area, and in their wanderings they might have left these tracks.

Then I realized that there was something like a path along the swamp. At first I wasn't sure, I thought it might be my imagination,

77

but in a few minutes there could be no more doubt. I broke into a run.

I followed the path for quite a distance. and finally broke out of the jungle into a clearing. And then—it wasn't a dream, it was really here! There in front of me I saw three little thatched huts and a colored man in shorts and a dirty brown shirt. Then I saw that there were also a colored woman and two children sitting under one of the shelters. The man was eating something. Then he looked up and saw me.

We stared at each other for about a minute. We were each appraising the other. I don't know what passed through his head but I will admit that he had some damn good reason to mistrust me. I must have been quite a sight. I had a heavy growth of beard. A mosquito net hung over my face, my hair was matted and in my right hand I carried as wicked looking a knife as I have ever seen. As for the impression he made on me, I didn't know but what he might be a head-hunter, but I knew if he was, there would be one hell of a fight, for I wasn't going to be stopped now. Suddenly he smiled a little, and I came to and said, "Hello, there." He answered something that sounded like "Hello," and his grin grew broader. I relaxed. He certainly looked friendly.

He took me over to his little hut, and his wife smiled and offered me a little cup of coffee. It was a demitasse, but the coffee was strong and hot. Nothing had ever tasted better. We both started to talk, and I realized that the language he was addressing me in was French. I struggled to remember a few words from high school French, and managed somehow to get it over to him that I was a lost flier. It was probably my sign language more than my French that conveyed that idea. It did me good to talk to somebody, though. I told him that I had to get help and go back to see if I could find my crew.

He gave me a piece of bread, but my hunger wasn't as bad as my thirst. Then he gave me a glass of some kind of liquor. It just about knocked my head off, but it sure did warm me as it went down. He said he was part of a small tribe that lived on the other side of the mountain. I gasped as I heard this, for I realized that if I had had the strength to go straight across the swamp back there I would have missed both him and his village. This was the only settlement anywhere in that whole region. The Lord was sure with me on that one.

After we had exchanged a lot of conversation and I was somewhat refreshed, he put me in his canoe with his wife and kids. We started out toward his village.

François was the name of my rescuer. He was of medium height and

In a canoe of this type Harmon and his guides traveled by river and ocean to Cayenne, French Guiana.

very black, and his teeth were badly stained. He smoked constantly all the time that I was with him. He was very conversational.

We paddled up to the village dock, and a number of people were there to greet us. Somehow the word had traveled ahead that a strange bird-man had appeared out of the jungle. A welcoming committee was on hand. One of the young men who greeted me was the policeman, mayor, fire chief, and official law-giver all rolled into one for that area. He took me to his house and showed me a map he had on his wall, pointing out where we were. I had been lucky, for my guess on where we must have crashed had not been far off. This was thanks to Ed Wolf's fine job of navigation and to his having identified Devil's Island as we went over it. The nearest town was Cayenne, French Guiana. The nearest base was Paramaribo, Surinam.

We at once started to make plans on how to get out to Cayenne. I was told by the Gendarme, as the young official was known, that they had men from the community going to Cayenne about once a month for supplies. They would make a special trip this time for my benefit. I was anxious to get out in order to let my folks know I was safe, and the sooner I got out there the sooner we could get search parties to the scene of the crash.

Our plans made, I was given the freedom of the house and the wonderful relief of a hot bath and an outfit of clean, dry clothes. I wasted no time in shedding my tattered flying suit and soaked shoes. My feet were black with dirt that was ground right into the skin, for the swamp mush had gotten into my shoes, and I had not taken them off for five days. I scrubbed and scrubbed, but couldn't get the stain off my skin. After my bath I gratefully put on the clean clothing, which included one of the Gendarme's uniforms, and a pair of slippers. My feet were so swollen I couldn't have got them back into my army shoes.

The Gendarme's house was swarming with people who had come to see the strange visitor. After a short time he got them cleared out, and a hammock was made up for me on the porch. I sank into it and fell asleep at once. That hammock seemed better than the finest bed in the world, it was like heaven after the hard ground I had been sleeping on in the rain.

We had agreed to start out at about two in the morning in order to make Cayenne by six the next evening. I slept until about midnight, and then was awakened to consume a fine dinner of peas and fish. My appetite was not big, for my stomach had gotten adjusted to no food at all and could not suddenly get back to normal. I ate a good meal, though, and helped as much as I could with the preparations for the trip to Cayenne.

Before leaving, the whole town turned out to give us a send-off and to present us with little gifts of food for the journey. They seemed like pleasant people who wanted to help. We started out as scheduled. The boat was a small outrigger canoe. The party consisted of François, the Gendarme, an old fisherman and his wife, and myself. The wife went along to cook for us. The canoe was not uncomfortable, and the natives knew the route well. We took turns paddling the canoe, and the first part of it was a bit tough. Dense grass had choked the small stream, and it was not easy to paddle through it. François and the old fisherman would get out of the canoe and push it over the grass when the paddles were of no more use.

As we traveled we talked. It was strange to discover that these people from the back country of the jungle knew about the war and were keenly interested in the fate of France. They knew about their country being lost to Germany, and were anxious to see France restored to her place in the world. They were impressed by the number of planes that flew over the jungle on their way to combat. They considered the Americans as their friends and allies, and were glad to be able to help me because I was an American.

The sun came busting through the clouds and it was morning. Occasionally the sun would disappear and it would rain, but the women of the town had given us large woven hats that acted as umbrellas. After about five hours of struggling along, the stream widened. I was happy to think we were going downstream toward the ocean. Going downstream made our progress quick and not difficult. I was thinking about a million things, it seemed, as we went sailing down that river. I wondered what my folks were doing. I knew the family would be together, for in time of trouble they always rally to each other's support. Then from thinking of my family a thousand miles away my attention would come back to the present scene. I looked at the colorful birds darting about in the trees and wished I had my movie camera along. It did not seem like the same kind of jungle I had found such a nightmare as I crawled through it.

But after eight hours or so of this riding I began to feel restless. I kept asking the Gendarme how far we had yet to go. I know how fed up he must have got with that question, but he understood my anxiety and never failed to answer with a big smile.

As we approached the ocean the weather appeared to be getting rough. It looked as if a big storm was coming up. The old fisherman put up the sail on the boat and settled back to let the wind do the work. Looking at the ocean, I somehow didn't like the idea of tangling with it in our little craft. I had been told that we couldn't stay out on the ocean straight through to Cayenne, but must come back inland a bit and get there by way of a small river. The currents and rocks around Devil's Island were too dangerous to try to navigate them. The wind was getting more violent as we left the mouth of the river. Once or twice such a big wave caught the boat that I thought we would surely turn over, but the old fisherman was a good sailor and knew how to ride those waves. We passed Devil's Island and headed for a small cove. The ocean breezes were still strong and we didn't have to use the paddles. It was now near six o'clock, so I knew that our schedule was off. We crossed behind Cayenne and came up on the north of it. The town was dark and the wind was cold. At about eleven that night we docked at Cayenne.

The Gendarme had to change to his good uniform before entering the town, and that delayed us a little more. Then we proceeded to the American headquarters. French Guiana had just declared itself Free French two weeks before, so I was in luck again—two weeks earlier I would have been a prisoner of the Vichy government.

We walked along the street, my loyal rescuer François supporting me, for my feet were so swollen I could hardly stand on them. At last we came to the American headquarters and went in. We were met in front by a French Captain, who took me to the commanding officer, a Commander in the United States Navy. I went up to him, beard and all, saluted as smartly as I could manage, and said, "Lieutenant Harmon reporting, sir."

The Commander just about dropped. The flight surgeon was called for. Army and Navy efficiency went to work at once. I was questioned in detail about the crash, and within an hour they had a Dutch Captain there who knew the whole territory like a book. Once complete information had been obtained from me and a search party planned to leave the next day, my needs were considered. I was treated to a nice dinner and put to bed with quinine pills and mosquito ointment. That army cot certainly seemed good. For the first time I slept with real ease, knowing that the rescue party was arranged and that my folks would soon be notified that I was safe.

The next morning the search party really got organized. I went out to the flying field and met Colonel Dorney, who was the Commanding

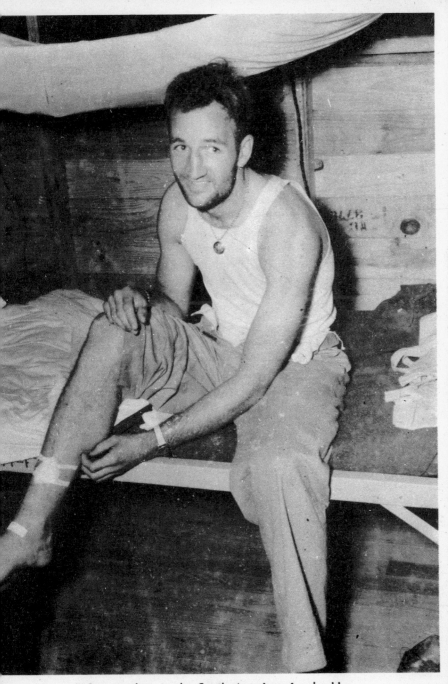
After six days in the South American jungle, Harmon has a good beard, is thirty-two pounds lighter.

Officer at Paramaribo. He had flown up to the new field at Cayenne in a B-18, and we were going out to search the vicinity for the wreck. I entered the bombardier's compartment in the nose of the ship and we started out. I had very little to go by except the little village and the small island I had stayed on one night. We flew over the town and then, after crossing a mountain or two, I saw the small island. I asked Colonel Dorney to take a heading due west and hold it. My line may not have been as straight as I tried to make it coming out, but it was our only chance of finding the ship. We held that course for about fifteen minutes and crossed right over the wreck of Little Butch.

The weather that day was bad and the visibility poor. We crossed the scene of the wreck and turned around. On the second pass we missed it, although it seemed we came back over the same area. The jungle was so dense that you had to be right on top of a thing like that wreck in order to see it. We circled and found Little Butch again, and the men in back took pictures of the crash. The weather was so bad that the pictures didn't turn out. We had the location of the crash all figured, though, so we returned to base. I was sent to the base hospital then and put to bed. I wanted to go with the search party, but the flight surgeon said nix. The search party left the next morning.

I stayed in the hospital while the search party were on their way to the plane. Anxiously I awaited news, but every day the story was the same. "They haven't reached the ship yet." After ten days, I was allowed to leave the hospital. The news of my escape had broken back home and wires were arriving from newspapers. It didn't appeal to me very much that all we had gone through should now amount to nothing but a good story for the boys from the press. And of course, what I was interested in right now was not publicity, but the safety of my crew. I hoped and prayed for them. Then, too, I had received orders from Washington that I wasn't to say anything to anyone about my story and all that had happened, and that naturally made it easier for me to be left alone.

General Walsh, the General in command of this area, came through a few days later. I was flown to Georgetown and saw him there. I told him I would be very happy if they let me rejoin my unit but first I would have to be given a chance to get outfitted again. I had not been able to salvage as much as a toothbrush from the crash. I had bought a new pair of pants and a couple of shirts. That was about all I had to my name.

General Walsh was on his way to Washington, so I was taken along as far as Florida. We landed at West Palm Beach and I was taken once more to the hospital. As soon as I arrived, I received a telephone call asking me when I was to go on the radio. I said, so far as I knew, never. That seemed to produce quite a sensation, for it had been broadcast all day that I would be on a coast to coast network that night. I don't know who had started the rumor, but anyway, I was under orders to keep quiet and that was what I was doing.

I tried to call home to Mom and Dad. I got Ann Arbor only to find that the folks had gone to Gary to be with the girls on Easter. I called Gary the next day, but then they had left to return to Ann Arbor. I succeeded in talking to my sister Sally though. I told her everything was all right and that I thought I could get home. I sure was counting my chickens before they were hatched that time.

I was placed under observation for four days. It was wonderful being in Florida. Everything seemed bigger than life and twice as natural. I was feeling pretty good, a little weak but coming back fast.

The fourth afternoon I was sunning myself on the beach when I received a call to report to the field. An officer came in and told me to pack my bag. I laughed and threw my two shirts and two pairs of pants into a bag—pack, indeed! We went to the field. I was taken to an office and handed an envelope. Inside this envelope were orders to rejoin my squadron.

I was not allowed to telephone my family, so I set about getting ready to go to Africa. The plane was to leave at midnight.

AFRICA

6

WHEN WE CLIMBED ABOARD the big transport my mind and heart were a million miles away. There was still no news from the search party that was out looking for the rest of the boys of the crew of Little Butch. I couldn't stop thinking about them. I wished I had been able to see the parents of the men of the crew. I couldn't have done anything to relieve their worry, but I could have told them about what had happened. I knew how those telegrams received from the War Department must have looked.

Fred Wieting's wife, Betty, was especially on my mind. She was due to have her baby soon, and that telegram wouldn't be any help to her. I remembered how much Fred had talked about his wife and how happy he was at the prospect of becoming a father.

There was an awful pain sort of all around in my chest, and I knew I would have to sit down and reason with myself, for there was nothing I could do about it and if I didn't snap out of it I would be of no use to anybody. Seeing my own folks might have helped me, but that was not in the cards. Besides, this was my own trouble and I had to work through it for myself. I had a job to do.

The big ship glided to a landing at Peurto Rico shortly after dawn. I was thankful that the stop was only long enough to refuel, and then we were off for Trinidad. I didn't want to see Peurto Rico again and be reminded of the fun the boys of Little Butch had had there such a short time ago.

On the plane I met and became fast friends with Major Robert Dean, who was with the transportation corps. He must have seen what was going on in my mind, for he seemed to be always at my side trying to cheer me up in a thousand little ways. The plane was full of military men bound for destinations in various theaters of action. They knew I had been over this route before and kept asking questions about every stop. I answered as best I could, although I hated to be reminded of it and it was still worse to have to talk about it.

Card games were started to kill the monotony of the long flights. In the large transports bad weather doesn't mean much. They are built for instrument flying and the crews are old airline men who are experts on that kind of thing. It is quite different from the tactical army planes where the reactions are so quick that sometimes the plane gets ahead of the instruments. The big transports of the Air Transport Command still have seats in them, just like in the old airline days. They are slower than the tactical ships, but much better in instrument weather. Their difference in speed isn't so great, but it is enough to make a difference, and you especially notice it in long flights.

After landing briefly at Trinidad we went on to Georgetown, where we stayed overnight. We prepared for an early hop to Belem. I didn't look forward to that hop again. What had happened the first time was still fresh in my mind. I had the utmost confidence in this big ship and its crew. They had flown this hop so many times, they knew it by heart. The transport command took the direct route instead of the coastal one, which made the trip shorter in time but meant the ship cut directly into the bad weather if it was there—and I have never heard of its not being there.

We took off at about four a.m. to get past the weather before it got too bad. The skipper of the big plane flew the whole way to Belem under the overcast. It was a rough ride but we arrived safely. His judgment was sound all the way, because he did not have to worry about any high mountain ranges on the route, and the weather we went through all day was quite calm, although it was raining and misty.

As we went along I tried to pick out the approximate spot where we had our accident, but we were too far inland to see the territory where Little Butch had gone down. I must say I felt a little better when we had reached Belem. It seemed as if the worst were now past and we would have clear sailing to Africa. I guess my thinking was getting ahead of me, for we still had the ocean to cross, but that was how I felt. I was also really glad to be getting back to my unit and to have the chance for action ahead of me.

Natal was our last stop before the hop across. We stayed overnight and one full day. Major Dean and I went into town together. It was supposed to be the best town along the entire route in South America. I wanted to try to get some clothing, for I had left the States with practically nothing to my name. I had had no chance to replace the kit I had lost, and was badly in need of a good many items. We found the boot shop which made the famous Natal boots that you can recognize anywhere from their distinctive cut. Whenever you see a guy with a pair of these boots on, you know that he has been through Natal. There just aren't any others like them. Major Dean and I each bought two pairs. I was still wearing a pair of old shoes I had borrowed from a lieutenant in South America, and since they weren't a very good fit I was delighted to get some new ones. The upper part of these Natal boots is made of good leather, and they later proved to be a godsend, for they protect the upper part of your legs fine in the desert country where you need it. The soles are like paper, or seem so after a little hard wear, but after all, a good pair of boots is a good pair of boots.

In Natal I ran into friends. Lieutenant Bill Ramsay was one of them. He was the pilot of a B-26 and was from my home town of Ann Arbor. Bill had had to make a crash landing at Georgetown due to a failure of the hydraulic line of his plane. He did a beautiful job with one of the Army's toughest ships, and got down without a scratch on any of his crew. The ship had been smashed up a bit, though, so they had to leave their plane and go over by transport. That meant Bill and I could stick together for the rest of the trip. Bill knew all about our crash. His had been one of the crews out in search of us. He knew how badly I felt about my crew.

In the following days we had great arguments about the relative merits of fighters and bombers. I had been a bomber pilot and thought highly of the B-25. If I was to remain in bombers, that would be the only ship for me. I liked the B-25, but always in the back of my mind remained the hope that I might tangle with a P-38. She was a swell fighter, and if you got hit it would be you and you alone who would take it. I had always thought the P-38 was the swellest looking ship in the sky, with her clean, smooth lines. And now I longed more than ever to be on my own.

Our discussions were great, and it developed that Bill really wanted a crack at the fighters too. I guess every bomber pilot feels that way once in a while. You feel that you would like to get into the cockpit of one of those fast little fighters and tear holes in the sky. Flying straight and level in a bomber is fine for guys of a certain temperament, but often a boy who would rather get all over the sky is placed in a bomber where he can't help but feel confined. I didn't know if I was reckless enough to qualify as a fighter pilot, for it takes quite a daredevil kind of make-up, but I certainly wanted to try.

The backlog of passengers waiting for transportation in Natal had built up. It wasn't a case of having low priorities, for Bill and his crew and I all had number one, but there were just too many number one priorities ahead of us. We finally got on a plane and started out for Ascension Island. It was dark when we took off, and I think both Bill and I showed a little nervousness. Pilots don't seem to worry when they are busy at their job, but let them be passengers and they "sweat out" every take-off and landing. We were in the air a couple of hours before the sun came up, and when it did we had our first glimpse of the middle of the ocean. We looked down, and there was nothing to be seen in any direction but vast stretches of the Atlantic. We were indeed a long way from home.

After a while we felt the big ship beginning to circle. I was sitting there hoping we would get to our destination as soon as possible, and now I thought maybe something was wrong and the pilot had decided to go back and not try to make it. The circle continued and we went around again. Then one of the plane's crew came back and told us they had contacted the survivors of a B-26 that had gone down around this area the day before. They were in a tiny raft and had a portable wireless set. The pilot asked all the passengers to help out by keeping a sharp lookout as we circled looking for them. Like all the rest of the passengers, I glued my eyes sharply on the ocean. I think my eyes were just about falling out with my effort to scan the surface of that waste of water, for it hadn't been long ago that I had been practically in the same situation as those guys down there.

We searched the area methodically for two hours. We knew that was the most that our fuel supply would permit as we swung back into our course and headed for our destination. I wondered how close we had come to those boys out there, and thought how terrible it was if we had passed fairly close and missed them. I knew from experience what their feeling must be if that happened. I could imagine them waving and yelling frantically at the sight of that speck in the sky, with an upsurge of jubilation at the thought of rescue. And then that sunk feeling as the plane pulls off into the distance and disappears. Thinking about those boys out in the ocean made me think of my own crew again and how some of them must be still wandering around in the living hell of the jungle. I said a silent prayer then that rescue might come to all the boys who were lost, and I asked the Lord with my whole heart that the war might be ended as soon as possible.

General Sherman certainly knew what he was talking about when he said "War is hell." He must have been thinking not only of those who do the fighting, but of all who must sit at home and wait to hear news of their loved ones. I couldn't help thinking of the families of these boys who were down. For the folks back home it's often harder than for us who have been trained to do the rough work.

We came down at Ascension Island, and I could see why it was called "The Rock." It's just the way you imagine Gibraltar must be. All the installations are hacked out of solid rock—army camps and defense works and so on. It is one of the most desolate places in the world, and I was glad that we were just going to stay there over night. Ascension is only a small island, just a pin point on the map in the midst of the vast stretches of ocean, but it has been developed into a mighty useful pin point in this war. It has been one of the main reasons that America has been able to "get there first with the most" in the matter of airplanes.

We might have gone on with only a brief stop at Ascension except for the hours that had been spent in our vain search for the fliers who were down, but the stop over night didn't make much difference in our schedule.

We went to a movie that night, and this was a big treat, we were informed by the boys on the island. Not very many pictures get there. The theater was an open amphitheater hacked out of the rock, like everything else on the island. You brought your own seat—there were no furnishings except the big screen down in front. Bill Ramsay and I went together. His tall, six-foot four length of good-humored frame, topped with a shock of light hair, lounged into that theater just like it was a piece of home. He made things seem natural and like good fun, and under the influence of his clowning around and wise-cracking I was beginning to feel more like my normal self than at any time since our crash.

At the show I ran into a classmate from flying school who was feeling upset because one of the bombers in his flight had run into trouble that afternoon. He told me the story. Shortly after their take-off from the rock, that bomber had lost an engine and tried to turn back. It was at a low altitude to start with and now it was losing altitude so fast that there was not time enough for the crew to throw off much of the heavy load they had on board. They went into the ocean about five miles off the island. The pilot was rescued after he had been in the water for three hours, and he was now in the hospital suffering from shock. His story was as follows. When the engine cut, he ordered everything thrown out in order to try to keep the big ship in the air. The bomb bays were jettisoned and the two enlisted men were busy throwing out everything that wasn't tied down. But the bomber went into the ocean in a crash landing. It stayed afloat a few seconds, then went down. The pilot, who had not been injured in the crash, floated out the top escape hatch. He had seen the co-pilot, who had forgotten to fasten his safety belt, thrown against the windshield. The pilot was swimming around in the water when the co-pilot's body came to the surface; he had apparently been killed immediately in the crash. His blood was all over in the water and the sharks came around right away. The pilot was treading water about twenty yards away while the sharks were tearing apart the body. More and more sharks came, and they would hit the pilot's legs with their fins trying to draw blood, but not attacking. He tried to fold up in as small a ball as possible to keep the sharks away, but this was difficult to do and still keep afloat. He went through three hours of this before the rescue boat reached him and pulled him in. The two enlisted men never were found at all.

After the show Bill and I went back to our tent. Once again we talked about the relative merits of fighters and bombers, and we were still talking when Bill dropped off to sleep. I must say I didn't have an easy time getting any sleep that night.

Once again at four a.m. we hit the runways for a take-off. Today we would reach Africa, and we felt that dark continent we had heard so much about was very close. I was eagerly awaiting the sight of it. We had an uneventful flight, and ran into a heavy haze about an hour off the African coast. We sailed right in and came down at our base on schedule. Later on, a pilot who had made the flight many times told me the haze was made up of dust blowing out from the continent in a great cloud.

This was my first sight of a real scene of war. All around the airport were big craters where shells from American warships had torn into the airport during our attack. The hangars were full of shellholes, and on the ground you could still see remnants of German planes that had flown for the last time. The field was a mere skeleton, for it had been only a few months before that the Americans had made their initial landings.

The sun was trying hard to fight its way through the haze that hung over the field, and the heat was sticky. Fine dust stuck to your skin and made your hair stand up like bristles on a brush. After supper, Bill and I went to another show. Last night we had seen a movie out in the middle of the Atlantic, and tonight we were calmly going to see one in Africa. The night was cool, and my clothing was light. I didn't have anything to speak of in the line of clothes, and nothing warm to put on. We sat out in the open theater and watched the film. Bill remarked, "That baby really stinks. If possible it's even worse than 'Harmon of Michigan.'" That was the only laugh we got out of the picture. The dust-haze still hung in the air and made the screen hard to see. We were sorry we hadn't just stayed in our barracks and got our sleep.

In the morning we were once more on our way. Our destination was Casablanca. The wind currents going across the desert were really wicked, and no one was sorry when we hit our first stop. It was Marrakech, and it was a pretty sight from the air. We had been flying over nothing but desert when suddenly we came to this white town set in the midst of green foliage. It looked like heaven. Marrakech is protected by a range of mountains, which is the reason it is so green and beautiful right in the middle of the desert. We checked in at the office for transient officers and were assigned rooms. As usual, I looked eagerly for the supply base, for I hoped sooner or later to get to a place where I could buy something to cover my back a little more decently. I found, however, that Marrakech wasn't the place either.

It was in Marrakech I ran into Lieutenant Dick Johnson from Michigan. He was a close friend of Ed Frutig, Michigan's All-American end. He proceeded to show me the town, and my short stay there was swell. It seemed good to see a face from home in this far away land. I was later to find that most of my friends and classmates were overseas, and no matter what distant post you hit you were likely to have the joy of meeting up with familiar faces. Our class was certainly well represented in the real war.

The next day we took off for Casablanca. This would be our last flight for a while, and we were waiting for our first sight of the town with some anticipation. We had all heard a great deal about Casablanca and how our boys had gone in there for the initial landings in the North African campaign. We had also seen a movie called "Casablanca," a very nice show, but it should have carried a note saying, "Any resemblance between the town of Casablanca in this picture and the real town it represents is purely coincidental." The city looked very good from the air. The buildings were all white and it looked clean and attractive.

After we had landed and checked in, Bill and I went to the operations office to find out where we were supposed to go. We were told that in a few days we would be taken out to the Bomber Base where the combat crews are 'processed.'

We checked in at the "De Gink" hotel at the field and then started into town. We wanted to see Casablanca for ourselves. There were Arabs everywhere, and one of the first things that struck us was the smell. It was everywhere around the Arabs. The French shops were all closed, as it was one o'clock and the French all go home at noon for a couple of hours. It was quite a revelation to me, and I felt I was learning about foreign countries fast. We succeeded in locating the American Post Exchange, where we secured toilet articles and cigarettes. Slowly but surely my stock of the necessities of life was getting built up. Outside the Post Exchange there were groups of small street Arabs. They knew only a few words: "Hey, Joe, gimme candy-shoeing gum pleze!" They were always after the soldiers on the streets. At first I was amused, but I soon got hardened to them like all the other soldiers. They were little nuisances, and most of the time you felt like batting them on the ear.

We had heard a great deal about the famous French wines, so we started out to sample some. That turned out to be not such a hot idea, but we drank it to show the proprietor that our hearts were in the right place. I hope that wasn't real French wine that we got!

It was in this little street cafe that I suffered one embarrassing moment. I had asked the bartender where the little boys' room was, and he pointed out a door marked W.C. I found out later that meant Water Closet, but for all I knew then it might be the abbreviation for 'Men' in Arabic. I stepped in and looked around. The room was empty, so I proceeded about my business. A second later the door opened and I turned my head to give a casual glance. Then I jumped. Standing behind me was a French gal. I must have got into the Ladies' by mistake! I was so embarrassed, I just about ruined the only clean pair of pants I had. I tore out of that door as fast as I could, past the girl who was as calm and collected as anything. I could feel how red my face was. When I got back to the table Bill asked me what the trouble was, and I told him. Bill just about fell off his chair laughing, and I wondered what was so darn funny about a trying moment like that. Then I was informed that a john is a john in these parts, and separate conveniences aren't provided for ladies and gentlemen. My mistake had just been not locking the door. Well, we live and learn.

After touring the town all afternoon, I felt I had seen about all of Casablanca I wanted to see for the present. It looked filthy and degraded to my eyes, and I felt a million miles from home. Nothing was familiar, it was all strange and not wonderful. It was in a mood of considerable dejection that we returned to our base that night.

Our spirits rose somewhat as we joined in with the rest of the gang in a song the British had taught us, "I've got sixpence, jolly, jolly sixpence," we sang. The sound of our voices ringing out in unison cheered us, and we felt better before we turned in for the night.

THE FIGHTER TRAINING CENTER

7

I HAD A CHANCE to talk to a lot of pilots during the two days I spent at the field in Casablanca.. The majority of these boys had seen combat service. We talked for the most part about the relative merits of bombers and fighters, and since their opinions ranged from one extreme to the other, they did nothing to change my mind. I was more than ever anxious to be transferred to the fighters.

Late in the afternoon of the third day, Bill and I received word that we were to report at the Bomber Training Center, which was located near Casablanca. I went to the Commanding Officer and asked him for permission to have a few days more to try to get together some clothes, for I had neither flying duds nor ordinary clothes sufficient to start a tour of duty. I was granted the extra day or so that I would need.

The next morning Bill and his crew left for the base. I was sorry to see them go. That day I traveled up to the headquarters of the training detachment. General Cannon, the General in command of the area, had his offices in the same building, I had been told, and the thought of it was drifting aimlessly in and out of my mind as I stood outside the guard rails of the offices. Then I became aware that an argument was going on. A full Colonel was in friendly dispute with a Major and two Captains. From the way the argument was going, it sounded as if everyone except the Colonel was a bomber pilot. I entered into the discussion on the Colonel's side, in defense of the fighters. Fortunately, the bomber they were talking about was the B-25, and I did have some experience with that ship. The argument continued, and the fighters now had better odds because of my having joined in on the Colonel's side. When the argument was all over, the Colonel asked me what was on my mind. I replied that I was trying to get permission to fly to one of our other bases in search of a supply of clothing, both flying and regular army wear, to complete my kit. Then he asked about my reason for arguing for fighters although I was a bomber pilot. I explained that I thought the world of the B-25, but that I would rather fly alone. After a few more questions from him, I wound up by telling him my whole story. He was very much interested and asked me if I would go with him to General Cannon and repeat what I had said. I gulped at the thought of telling my story to a general, but said of course I would be glad to.

The Colonel took me over to the General's headquarters, and after I had told my story, the Colonel added that I would like to fly a fighter. General Cannon asked me: "Harmon, don't you think you would be a better man in bombers now because of your experience?" I replied, "I don't know, sir, that might be. But my crew before meant the world to me, and I would feel better flying alone now, if I could." The General then turned to Colonel Allison and told him to take me out to the Fighter Training Center and tie a P-38 on my tail and "see what happens."

When I heard those words, I just about turned cartwheels. Getting the chance to fly a P-38 would mean everything to me. I hadn't known I could feel so relieved and happy again.

The next day I flew to the other base and picked up a few things to fly with. Colonel Allison took me over to the parachute shop, where I got a new chute. After my last experience, that was one little item I wanted to be sure was perfect, although I hoped I wouldn't have to use it again.

It was a hot drive the next day out to the Fighter Training Center, but I was too anxious to get there to pay much attention to the weather. I had dreamed so long about flying a P-38 that now it was hard to believe that my chance had really come. Colonel Allison turned me over to Lieutenant Colonel Jones, the Commanding Officer at the center. He was very young to be a Colonel and, I was to find out soon, as hard a worker as I have ever known. I was assigned to a tent in the area and began to get acquainted with the center.

The Fighter Training Center was a great institution. I guess that just about every famous flier in the African theater has passed through it. Above the main gate is a sign which reads: THRU THESE GATES PASS THE BEST DAMN FIGHTER PILOTS IN THE WORLD. That was one of Jonesie's ways of keeping up morale. As a matter of fact, the sign told the literal truth, I am sure. Jonesie, as the Colonel was almost always called, was very well liked, and everyone knew he was an excellent commander. One of his main interests was the safety of the fliers who were under his jurisdiction, and breaking one of the rules of flying safety was a major offense. The center was pretty new as yet, and there weren't many buildings. The main offices, mess hall, and school buildings were the only barracks. The pilots lived in tents.

Pilots of all types of fighter planes were there on the post, housed in the same area. There was a great rivalry between the pilots who flew the different ships, P-39's, P-38's, P-40's and Spitfires. The Spitfire boys would always be calling us names like "push-button pilots," and we would always come back with some quip such as that they were "bouncing baby-carriage drivers." The arguments about the relative merits of the planes went on constantly.

The school was founded on the theory that pilots should get the latest information on tactics and a thorough knowledge of the enemy methods before going up to the front. The day was divided into two

95

periods. Half of the day you went to school, the other half you flew. The instructors were men who had just returned from the combat zone and could teach you the latest tricks. It was a great set-up and you had to work hard. The system was a great help to all the new pilots, for it kept them from going into a combat outfit cold. It got them in trim, often after quite a period of not flying due to the long trip over, and gave them a chance to work with real combat instructors. It put the final polish on their preparation for the real thing.

I was placed in a tent with two P-39 pilots. They were great guys, although on the surface they acted like the world's laziest. At this time the P-39's were not being used very much, and these two fellows had gone through school together and had been at the center almost as long as the instructors. They knew all the ropes.

My first meeting with one of the P-38 pilots had taken place a few nights before at the Officers' Club in Casablanca. There I had run into a boy by the name of Bob Schultz. Bob had formerly been a P.R.U. man, which means Photo Reconnaissance Unit, and had flown a P-38 without guns on reconnaissance flights. When I met him, he had just flown a P-38 from England down to Africa. Bob was an Ohio State man, having attended the buckeye school at the same time I was going to Michigan. For some reason he was called "Schlitz" or "Bruce" most of the time, I never did know why. He is one of the most likable eggs in the world, always laughing and clowning with a carefree attitude.

At our meeting, Bob told me he had heard a hot "Latrine-o-gram" (army slang for rumor) that there was going to be a ferrying job to take some P-38's up to Russia. He was all for making the trip, and I sort of envied him, because I wouldn't have minded seeing Russia myself. But a day or two later I found out that his rumor had been nothing else but, for who should I see putting his things in the tent next to mine at the Fighter Center but good old Schlitz! I razzed him then, and he took it good-naturedly, as he always does. This was the start of a friendship that was to last all through combat. I always had a picnic with Schultz, because he was always razzing me, and I seldom missed on handing it back. When the razz got a little bit hot, I would always clinch things by referring to the football scores of Michigan versus Ohio State. That would usually put the stopper on him. We used to go everywhere together. One of his great themes was his prowess with the ladies, but during all the time I knew him and was with him, I never knew him to have a date. He had a great time trying to make me believe some of his "tall ones."

The flying at the center was hot and heavy. Schultz and I were placed in a flight with Major Bob Kirtley. Kirtley was the commanding officer of a squadron of a Fighter Group, and had had his outfit on the front line when the going was tough. He had led his squadron against the famous "yellow nose" squadron of the Germans, and if you have heard anything at all about that outfit you know it was tough. Kirtley's record at the front was one to be envied, for he had accomplished all his missions and seldom lost a man. His reputation always traveled ahead of him. For example, he was known always to be the first man in his flight to help out any member of the squadron who happened to get into things a little too deep for comfort. What he couldn't do with a P-38 just wasn't worth talking about. I think he was the finest P-38 combat pilot I have even known. He was small in stature, with sandy red hair. His men would have followed him to hell and back and would have taken on Satan and his mob at their own level. He knew every man in his gang, and if the man needed it, Kirtley would be right in there standing up for him, even if it meant an argument with a four-star general.

There was nothing particularly striking about my first meeting with this officer I had heard so much about, but it will always stand out in my memory. I was on the flight line fooling around with Schultz when somebody came along with Major Kirtley and I was introduced. He asked me about my previous flying time, and I told him I had flown the B-25 quite a bit. He seemed glad to hear that, and said, "You should have no trouble with a P-38, then." There was nothing special about this interchange, but the picture of his keen, rather sharp features and the wiry kind of strength he had remain with me.

He gave me the Tech orders on the P-38. He pointed out one of the planes on the ground and told me to climb in and familiarize myself with the cockpit. I took the big book he handed me and went on my way. The cockpit of the P-38 was very compact, I found. It was quite different from the set-up in a bomber, where some of the instruments are out of reach. I had been in the ship about an hour when Kirtley came over. He climbed up on the wing and said, "Well, are you ready?"

I just about choked as I said, "Ready for what, sir?"

He replied, "There's the runway," and I just about choked again, I was so excited. I didn't have any idea of getting to fly the ship so soon. I started the engines and taxied out. The sensation of your first flight in a P-38 after flying a bomber is indescribable. I'll never forget that moment. In a P-38, you have take-off power the minute you release the brakes, while in a bomber you have to start rolling to pick up speed. The only thing I can think of to describe that surge of motion you get when you let go of the brakes is that it is like having somebody hit you hard on the fanny with a snow-shovel when you're a little kid. You simply go sailing. That's the way I went down that runway, and the trim little ship jumped into the air. I felt like a million dollars.

My first flight lasted about two hours. I took the ship up to a good altitude and felt her out. She handled like a dream, she was simply wonderful. I took her through a good many paces that afternoon, but knew I hadn't even begun to find out what she was capable of. I felt like a new man when I landed. When I came into the pilots' room, some of the boys asked me if I didn't think she was a little heavy on the controls. I just laughed. To me she was lighter than a feather, after flying a bomber. Schultz was there with congratulations, and from that day on our work was cut out for us.

The flight Kirtley had at the base was made up of instructors who had been in his squadron up at the front. They were Lieutenants Yaney, Jones, Hattenforf, and Walker. A few days after we arrived at the base they were awarded medals for their achievements at the front. They were a great gang, and the students who flew with them learned a lot. I know I did. Schultz and I flew together quite often, and he was always clowning around up to the moment he climbed into the cockpit. After that he was a different man.

It was just about a ritual for Schultz and me to go into town together on Monday afternoons. That was the day that a little French shop in Casablanca had ice cream. They saved their rations all week in order to make it this one day. It wasn't like ice cream at home, but it was darn good. We would eat four or five dishes of it every Monday afternoon, and it was a real treat. The little shop did a lot for French-American friendship.

Schultz and I were always getting around to one thing and another. One night we were invited in to Casablanca to an Arab wedding. The bridegroom was one of the waiters in the mess hall of the Air Corps hotel. The festivities were already in full bloom when we got there, and all the officers from the Air Corps hotel were present. Schultz and I got right into the middle of the party. We sat on the floor with our knees folded under us regular Arab fashion. The show consisted of several dancing girls who danced to the music of a couple of flutes and some drums. It was very mystical sounding music, and the contortions those girls went through in their dance were something for our book. One of the dancers danced a whole dance with a tray of filled glasses on her head and never spilled a drop of all that liquid. Her movements were all from the waist down and very precise and controlled. All the time that we were watching the entertainment and enjoying the festivities, the father of the bridegroom was serving hot minted tea. It tasted innocent enough, and Schultz loved it. As far as we could tell, it was non-alcholic. We found out differently, though, when we were ready to go home and tried to get to our feet. Schultz, who had imbibed freely, could hardly control his legs. We bummed a ride home to the base with Colonel Jones. Schultz and I sat in the rumble seat.

When we arrived at the base, Schultz had succeeded in getting down on the floor to keep out of the bitter cold night wind. I had quite a time pulling him out. I escorted him to his tent, and when we were within five feet of it I pointed to the doorway and gave him a slight push in the right direction. He walked straight away from the flap of the tent and around to the side. He walked right into the side of the tent, and pulled the whole thing, stakes and all, down on top of him. I practically fell down myself, I was laughing so hard. After fifteen minutes, Schultz was trying to get into the small hole that is left for ventilation at the top of the tent. It was too funny for words. It looked like the sort of thing you used to see in the old slapstick movies. We finally took pity on him and put him to bed. With that scene as the wind-up, we all had fond memories of the one Arab wedding we ever attended.

Life went on at the training center and we piled up flying time. Often we went on ferry trips to take new ships up to the front for the combat squadrons. These trips were exciting. Often we could see the damage our forces had inflicted when they landed and took over. Airports everywhere were still torn up, all except the runways. These had been put back into shape immediately. Going up to the front like that we got a sort of preview of what was to come for us. We saw the evidence of bombing missions by the Germans and at times we were in them. If we ever had any doubts we were now convinced that the jerries would give you all the work you could handle in the sky. They were putting up a fierce fight and we would soon be in it.

At this time one of the new friends we made was Major "Pat" Patton of the training center. He had been a physical education instructor at an Arizona Park before the war, and sort of felt like a father to every pilot who came to the center.

Now the Americans were getting to the point where they could throw real strength into the air against the Germans. Before this time, the odds had generally been against us. While we were in Oran on a trip one day we ran into a couple of German prisoners at the airport. They were pilots of Goering's famed *Luftwaffe*, who had been shot down on a recent raid in that area. They looked like clean-cut boys. I guess their age was about nineteen. While we were waiting around the airport we talked to them. They spoke quite good English, and they neither looked nor sounded like Hitler's terrible supermen we had heard so much about. They were just young boys with a fanatical belief in their mustachioed little chief. They talked long and loudly about how Germany was certain to win the war. We asked them if Germany's recent defeats didn't mean anything to them, and they replied, "Germany has only made a strategic retreat as part of its high strategy. Certainly the United States cannot hold out much longer with her country in shambles and her ships all being sunk by our submarines." This last statement just about threw me, because from where we stood we could see hundreds of ships steaming in and out of the harbor. It was certain that these were not German ships. I pointed to them and said, "Does that look as if all our ships are being sunk?" They could not gainsay that many ships were certainly getting through, and the sight of the traffic in the harbor there obviously astonished them. However, they still maintained that New York City was all bombed to bits. It just happened that there was a picture of the New York skyline in that day's newspaper. I showed it to them, saying, "That picture was taken only a few days ago." They wouldn't believe it. They insisted that it was only propaganda.

After a while we had to leave for our planes. I thought a good deal about those two young fliers when we got back to the base, and I was thankful I was an American. I felt sure of one thing, and that is that Americans talk, write and feel as they damn well please. No organized propaganda has told us what we have to believe.

I also felt we were learning quite a lot about our enemy in such encounters as this. A few days later we again went on a ferry trip, and it gave us the opportunity to hear firsthand one of the best war stories I know about. We landed at one of the advanced P-38 bases where the Germans had made a raid that morning. In the fight that took place then, quite a few jerries had been shot down. One of these boys was a full Colonel in the German Air Force. He had the yellow nose on his ship that designated him as nobody's fool in the air. According to rumor, the yellow-nose boys have to have fifty victories to their credit. Whether that is true or not, and that figure certainly sounds pretty high, the yellow noses have always proved the toughest in combat. While Intelligence officers were questioning the German colonel, it seems, the young pilot who had shot him down entered the room. The colonel saw the pilot and just spat in his face with rage. It was lucky that there were several men in the room, or there would have been one less German to take to prison camp. After the pilot had cooled down, the German was told that his manners were indeed very bad, and that this was the pilot who had shot him down. The German at once apologized and was loud in his praise of the flying the American pilot had done to get him. He said he had some seventy victories to his credit, and no doubt the young Second Lieutenant had at least as many. The American pilot had simmered down a bit, and laughed as he drawled, "Well, let's see, I have shot up one German outhouse, one Arab on a camel, by mistake, and you." That piece of information just about threw the German, but it was a fact. It was the first victory for the young American and only his second ride on missions.

When we arrived back at our base, Schultz and I found out from Major Patton that we were on alert to go up to the front. The rumors had it hot and heavy, because there were just ten men designated to go with this batch. Major Patton told us that we would not be fighting in this area, and we were worried. It sounded like something real, but it left plenty of room for speculation about where we were to be sent. The men who had been selected were quite happy because we were going to get into action somewhere or anywhere. Our happiness was increased when we learned that Major Kirtley was going to be our new Commanding Officer on the deal. So far as we were concerned, that made things look like pure gold.

A few days later we got the full dope on the job. We were to be the first group of P-38's to fight in China under General Claire L. Chennault. Eagerness to get going was visible on every man's face. The ten men who were going were Arpin, Beardsley, Machado, Newnom, Opsvig, Longueil, Weber, Yorsteon, Schultz and me. We spent the next few days getting set. It was going to be a great adventure for sure! From intelligence reports we heard, among other things, that the Japs were still using their obsolete planes, but obsolete or not, we thought with pleasure of what our P-38's would do to them.

We were to pick up our planes in North Africa and fly them over to China, according to arrangements. That would be the longest flight we had heard of by an Army Fighter Squadron. Schultz and I were still together, and we were glad we were going to get a chance to fight the Japs. The Germans are our enemies all right, but we thought we would, if anything, rather fight those dirty Japs. After their backstabbing deal at Pearl Harbor, they were our personal fight. Fighting the Japs under Chennault with Kirtley leading, what could possibly be a better prospect than that! The night before we were to leave, there was little thought of sleep for any of the ten. So far as we were concerned, tomorrow couldn't come soon enough.

THE BIRTH OF SQUADRON X

8

IT WAS LATE IN the afternoon of a July day. The African sun beat down upon the desert with the force of a sledge hammer. Schultz and I were standing in front of the administration building. We had all our things packed and were ready to go. We were talking about how we hated to say goodbye to everyone. We had made many real friends here at the Fighter Training Center, and now the time had come, as it always does, to push off.

Three years ago we had been deadly rivals. We didn't know each other personally, but the most important thing in life we had to worry about then was the score of the Michigan-Ohio State football game, and our hopes didn't exactly call for the same results. Now we were as close buddies as you could find, and our worries were considerably more serious. Bob and I were both midwesterners, and when you get very far away, Ohio and Michigan seem pretty close together. Our homes were a lot alike, and we had the same kind of background. The farther you get from home, the more it means to you being with other Americans, and especially being with a pal from your own part of the country. I was thinking about a small white house in Ann Arbor, and wishing I could get home to see it again soon, and I guess Bob was thinking about his home in Sandusky, Ohio. We were both simply champing the bit to get going on our assignment to China, but still, here we were standing around thinking about home. I guess that is how it is with all the boys. Every time they are about to get going on a new move, they spend the last hours before starting out thinking about things.

I was thinking about home, and then about America. I have often tried to find a definition for America, but it's a hard job whether you have a college degree or not! I read once in a magazine that America meant Apple Pie. That seemed kind of silly, but in a way it was as sensible as anything else you could pin it down to. You needn't explain why you like it and why you can't imagine life without it. It's simple and good and wholesome. It means home, and then it means the ones you love, and the thrill of a football game in the fall with the stadium full and the boys running out on the field and the bright colors in the bleachers, and it means taking your sweetheart to the Junior Prom all dressed up and looking so pretty you are prouder of her than ever, and the campus all white with snow in the middle of the winter, and standing in front of the library chewing the fat with the boys—and you say Apple Pie. Okay. That's what Bob and I were thinking about. America, that great and varied thing we couldn't describe but were proud and eager to fight for.

We felt we were part of the mighty American machine. We got quite a thrill out of the feeling that the wheels were about to get moving, that our part of the machine was going to function. And of course we were glad that what we were going to do was fight in the P-38. Being a cog in a machine is great if you have the luck that we did. We were flying a plane we were crazy about. Right that afternoon we were going to start by truck for Casablanca, where we would meet the rest of the boys that were to make the long flight to China together.

The chips were down, and we would have to use every bit of skill we had learned during our training to come out on top. The thought of actual combat made us set our jaws a little more firmly. We knew there would be a lot of action between the present and the time we got back to those homes we stood and dreamed about for a few minutes in front of the administration building, but we hoped, with God's help, to get back there some day and take up again where we had left off.

Bob wasn't a Catholic, but early that evening he went to Mass with me. He may not have understood the Catholic religion, but services were services to him. He had real faith in the Big Boss upstairs, and though it would have been as hard for him as for me to define that belief, he knew in his heart, as I did, that getting back home safe and sound would depend a lot on the Boss's help. I received communion and my prayer was that we would both be given the help and guidance we needed.

As the sun went down over the ridge that evening, the ten boys who were about to leave sat around joking. The sound of a heavy Army truck approaching brought a sense of immediacy to the gathering. Our transportation had arrived. The bags went in first, we followed and off we went. We were on our way to Casablanca to meet the rest of the squadron.

Major Kirtley had been busier than a one-armed paperhanger getting the last minute arrangements set. We were to travel as a squadron, taking every bit of our supplies along with us. Our crew chiefs, the enlisted men who were our planes' mechanics, had gone on ahead and we would meet them in India. They were veterans of the African campaign, men who knew what makes the P-38 tick. There was not a thing about her from propeller to aileron that they didn't know. For this we were very thankful, for we knew only too well, as many a newspaper reader back home doesn't, that behind every pilot who shoots down an enemy plane there must be a top-notch ground crew of three or four men who have just as much a part in the victory as the fellow up there who presses the trigger. Together we would make a deadly team, but alone we wouldn't be much use.

The thought of the crew chiefs having gone ahead to India didn't exactly make us feel happy, for that meant that we would have to be our own ground crews, more or less, over some 8,000 miles of flying. It would be a tricky business. To make matters worse, we were told that anybody who dropped out because of a mechanical failure of his ship would have to return to Africa and be left out of the trip. Looking at the faces of the pilots when that statement was read out, you could see that every man on the flight was resolved to fly his ship to its destination, by the seat of his pants if necessary. Some of us practically had to do just that, as things turned out.

At the Casablanca airport we met the bulk of the squadron. It was made up of volunteers from the three P-38 Fighter Groups in action on the African Front. We all pitched in and helped Major Kirtley, and thanks to the comradeship of hard labor we got acquainted fast. The men were all young, and many had seen quite a bit of hell-for-leather flying. The others, inexperienced like myself, hoped to learn from the combat boys. We spent about two days in Casablanca, where we picked up some of our planes, and then went on to Algiers, where we were to get the rest. Last minute preparations were to be made in Algiers, and when we left there we would really be on our way.

We stayed several days in Algiers, for we had to have a change in radios and there were many other things to be done. The second day we were there, Major Kirtley made the assignment of planes. We had been given new planes, but some had been slightly damaged, so we drew numbers out of a hat to see who would get which. The ole Harmon luck held out and I drew one of the latest model P-38's. That afternoon when Schultz and I went out to the airport to locate our planes and start working on them we were full of expectation. I was anxiously looking forward to the first sight of the ship that I knew would be called "Little Butch II." After considerable running around I finally found her. A few days previous she had been rammed by a transport, but after a new rudder was put on the right side she was just like new. In fact, she was darn new. Checking the form number one, the army's individual record of each ship, I found she had only eight hours on her. When I crawled into the cockpit, I was the proudest man on earth. I had my own P-38.

There were probably about two hundred other P-38's out there on that field, but there was no other as pretty as mine. I don't know what the difference was, but "Little Butch II" just had it and plenty of it.

Our squadron had a number one priority on work, for we were regarded as a rush job. I succeeded in getting my ship into a hangar the next morning, and we went to work on her. She had been sitting out on the field for some time, and the dust thrown up by other planes landing and taking off nearby had given her a foot-thick coating. I appointed myseh a committee of one to give her a good bath. I spent the next two days working hard as a warhorse, scrubbing her with used gasoline, that is, gas that has been drained from other ships, and I sure found out that the P-38 is a pretty big plane as I went over every square inch of her. When I had finished, she was slick as grease and shining like an angel. After getting the tail fixed, we took off for our first flight together. Butch and I were beginning to get acquainted. That bath I had given her really got results, for we slipped through the air like a real bolt of lightning. I knew then why the P-38 was called the "Lightning."

During our stay in Algiers the men of our squadron really got to know one another. It was an unusual squadron in many respects. All the men had volunteered for this long and difficult operation. It was the first combat group to be formed in one theater of war in order to be flown to fight in another. We were about to make the longest pursuit flight on record for an Army squadron, and ours would be the first P-38's to take to the air against the Japs in China. Every man in the outfit was mighty glad to be a part of it. You could tell that from the undercurrent of pride in their talk. These twenty-five men were to form the finest band of friendship that I have ever seen. Loyal and cohesive, they were to have many laughs and good times together in the coming months. They were to witness death together and remain outwardly impassive. Much would happen to them, but for the present everyone was eating and sleeping well, dreaming of China, and growing to think and feel as one group. It was easy to tell that the squadron was getting together.

I was a bit stiff from my workout on that washing job when I went out to the field the next morning. The rest of the boys had given me the horse laugh for working so hard, but if I was going to fly and fight in my plane I wanted to have her perfectly groomed and as pretty as could be, not to mention in perfect shape for action. I had just one job left to be done, and that was to get her name painted on her nose. That had to be done before I could take off, but otherwise I was all set.

I found a painter at the field and asked him if he would do the job for me. He said he would. He finished the job in three hours, and it was really first-rate. My insignia was drawn for me by Walt Disney, whom I had met when I was in Hollywood. It was a picture of "Peg-leg Pete," one of the Disney characters, dressed in a Michigan football suit with my number, 98, on it. That number meant a lot to me. I was positively superstitious about having it on my football jersey in the good old days and on my plane now. Peg-leg Pete was a funny guy to have there next to the name Little Butch, especially since he carried a sub-machine gun in one hand and was altogether a very threatening looking character. But few people besides myself knew that my plane was named for one of the loveliest and daintiest girls in the world.

Schultz was having quite a time trying to decide what to call his plane. He finally decided on the name "Golden Eagle." It had been the name of a sailboat he had sailed often on Lake Erie. It had swell memories for him. He didn't manage to get the same painter who had done my job, though. His painter must have been a guy with surrealist ideas. It was the worst painting I have ever seen. In one of the eagle's claws was a bottle, and in the other a swastika, indicating, I suppose that he was out to lick the demon rum as well as the Nazis. Schultz

Harmon and his P-38, Little Butch II.

thought his painting was beautiful, but the boys never gave him a second's peace about it. It couldn't possibly have been that the bird was drawing helpful encouragement from that bottle, could it?

One of the boys in the squadron whom we got to know first in Algiers was Ryan Moon. We had nicknamed him Moonbeam, because when our orders came out his name was spelled with an "m" at the end, and that had a crazy flavor to it. Moonbeam was a redhead from Oklahoma. He got along well with everybody because he was a natural born clown and was always having a great time and giving everybody else a great time too. He had a fine combat record in Africa and could pilot a P-38 through anything. Moonbeam was more or less appointed as general trouble-shooter by Major Kirtley. He was to see that everything was getting set on schedule at the field while the Major got the official business lined up. We got to know Moonbeam very well indeed before we left for China. He was second to none as a gambler. He would playfully cheat your backteeth out if he could, but everyone knew he was always clowning and he never could get away with it. When he was playing a game seriously, he was as rough an adversary over the poker table as he was in the sky, and that was a bundle to handle. It was to be his job to fly clean-up in the flight, which meant he was to be the last man and pick up anybody who had to stay behind because of motor trouble or something like that. The only trouble with Moonbeam as end man was that he usually had most of the squadron flying back there with him, not because they had motor trouble or anything, but just because everybody liked to fly with him.

We took about five days in Algiers, and then we were ready to push off. We had decided to move on to Tulergma the next day to form there and leave as soon as possible. The day before we were to leave we had quite a blow. Major Kirtley was taken from his job as Commanding Officer of the squadron and given the job of Executive Officer of the First Fighter Group. He was almost as disappointed as we were, for he wanted to stay with us and go to China, but his ability and experience had led to this new appointment that was supposed to be a bigger job. Captain Sam Palmer took over the squadron. He was the ranking man in the outfit, but very few of the men knew him because he had been away most of the time we were preparing to go. He arrived and we all got introduced. Captain Palmer had seen a lot of action at the front and knew what the score was, and in spite of our disappointment at losing Major Kirtley we all had confidence in him.

We left Algiers as "Squadron X," for as yet we had no official designation.

Although we thought we were completely set, there were still a few preparations to finish. The men were learning new things every day, at least I certainly was. I had been flying on Moonbeam's wing, and the redhead really knew his way around the skies. We had a meeting at Tulergma, and the method of flight from then on was explained to us. Rather than try to stick all together in one bunch, it was decided that we would form a number of smaller flights. In this way it would be less trouble to keep track of everybody. Moon would be flying the last flight so that any straggler would be picked up. I suppose we would attract less attention, too, flying in smaller groups rather than in one big one.

I was to be in a flight led by Earl Helms. Earl was a good-looking boy from Michigan. He had been flying in Africa, and I thought he could have been a model for a typical Fighter Pilot. He flew like a champion. He was always willing to tip me off about things and help me out, and I was grateful to him for it. In combat I had heard Helms flew like a madman. He was to be the first member of the squadron to get a Zero, and it was only two days after he hit China. He had a running fight with the Jap for about a hundred miles and finally shot him down in flames. In his enthusiasm he was so intent on getting that Jap that he went too far, ran out of gas, and had to make a belly-landing in a rice paddy. That was the typical Helms way of doing something. On the ground he was as easy-going as any man in the outfit, but in the air he was out for business—and that meant bad business for the Jap.

Well, the flights were all picked, and everyone was anxious to be on the way. At last. The night before we left Tulergma, Schultz and I sat outside our barracks chewing the fat as usual. The squadron was our topic of conversation, and we were comparing notes on the boys we had been getting to know and the impressions we had drawn from our meetings with them. It didn't take us long to come to the conclusion that we were in a real outfit. Those guys were the real stuff, and they knew an awful lot more about combat and flying than we did. Underneath our talk was always the realization that not all the members of our squadron could come through the fighting. It was too much to hope for that we all would be returning from this mission to China. I wanted to write Mom a letter before we left, so I went inside. The barracks were hot and stuffy and sleep was hard to get, anyway. My last sentences to Mom that night still stick in my memory. "Don't worry, Mom, I am going on a fine adventure. I have the good fortune to be with a bunch who are not only fine pilots, but fine men. Keep saying those Hail Mary's and I'll be home before you know it." That night as I wrote those words I had not the least doubt in my heart that they would come true. I felt secure, and had confidence not only in my own preparation but still more in the experience and ability of those men whom I had met such a short time ago but with whom I had been flying long enough to know they were tops. Beyond that, my deepest faith was always in the Big Boss upstairs, who had given it to me to be associated with this wonderful outfit.

Schultz and I, who were, relatively speaking, rookies on our job, knew that the men of Squadron X would make a real name for themselves in the skies over China before they were finished. And we were looking forward to the show.

THE TRIP TO CHINA

9

AT FOUR-THIRTY A.M. on the button, Captain Palmer started his engines. The first flight moved down the runway and took off. It was a beautiful sight as the flights followed each other. It reminded me a little of the movies, for there was almost something unreal about it. Planes taking off at dawn for an objective and spraying up a fine silt of African dust as they took to the air. Every ship got off on schedule that day except one that had to turn back. Moon was standing by to pick him up as soon as the failure was corrected. They were not able to take off until the following morning.

Little Butch sailed right into the air like a bird. Our flight plan was all made out, and every man knew where he was to land after this first day's flight. It would be a long haul of five hours. That many hours in a fighter really is something and no fooling. You can cover quite a lot of ground in that time in these fast little ships. After a five hour flight in the cramped quarters of a fighter plane, you really feel that you have covered territory, too. Sometimes you have to be pulled out of the plane bodily, because your legs have gone to sleep and have he prickles so badly they won't work, and there is nothing you can do about it—there's no room to stretch in a P-38 cockpit.

Leaving at four-thirty meant we would reach our destination early, before the hot African sun had much of a chance to overheat our engines. That sun is certainly a powerhouse. Flying over the desert is no picnic, and fighting over it must be a real man's job. I had thought about this often as we flew over the desert, but I always fell back on a bit of Coach Crisler's football philosophy. "It may be raining cats and dogs," he would say, "but remember, it's just as wet on the other side of the field." If the jerries could take that weather, our boys would have no trouble with it either.

This was my first experience of a long flight in a fighter, and I was to learn a lot by experience. Lessons taught in this way are always the easiest to remember. Little Butch purred like a kitten. I felt wonderful as we started out over the Mediterranean Sea. Our first flight was to take us to Bengasi. The squadron looked beautiful in formation as we crossed over the bomb torn cities of Sfax and Gabes. I had heard great tales of these spots. Major Kirtley had told us how hot it was over Gabes. The Germans have always been past masters at throwing up flak, and it seems that over Gabes they really put on a demonstration of what flak can be. The American planes did their best to dodge it, but no matter what, they came in anyway. We were now flying back over the route of Rommel's retreat before the forces of General Montgomery. It was easy to see from above that the course of War had passed there and left its mark in the destruction of harbors and towns in its path. From above you got a bird's-eye view of the whole thing, but I dare say it looked considerably worse from the ground.

We were briefed to keep along the coast of the Gulf of Sidra all the way to Bengasi, because if anything happened to one of the planes, the pilot could always make a belly landing on the beach. There was a bit of excitement that day, as Lieutenant Art Arpin blew an oil line and had to jettison the large belly tanks of extra fuel he carried. He managed to keep his ship in the air okay, but his loss of the belly tanks gave the flight trouble later on because he was unable to carry enough fuel for the long hops.

The British were in control at Bengasi and were always flying patrols around the city. We had been instructed to enter the city from a certain direction in order to be recognized, for otherwise we would have run some danger of being fired upon before we could be identified.

Our machine guns were loaded for business, too, for we never knew when a flight of the enemy might try to intercept us. The air was tense as we came into the corridor from the proper direction and a flight of Spitfires circled us. We gave them the colors of the day, the American recognition code colors, and passed their inspection. I know that every man in the flight let out a relieved sigh when that preliminary was over.

Captain Palmer was leading our flight and had a bit of trouble finding the right airdrome. We were to land at one of our heavy bomber bases. That is what we did, but it wasn't the right one. The B-24's had just taken off to hand Adolf and his lads a couple of crates of strictly fresh American made eggs. The field was a regular dust bowl, and the day was already hotter than Hades. Everyone was perspiring freely when we landed, and the brownish red dust that blew into the air every time a plane hit the ground stuck to us. There was a definite haze and visibility was bad. After we had climbed out of our ships, we went and had mess with the heavy bomber boys. The red dust was caked on our skin like clay. Our sympathy went out to those bomber boys whose home base was that field. We didn't envy them a bit. China was looking better and better to us.

After lunch, we decided to fly over to the field where we had been supposed to land. We got to another B-24 base. The boys there had better accommodations though. They had somehow managed to rig up a refrigerator and had cold drinks. Our flight must have created quite a drain on their lemonade and orangeade supplies, for we all drank as if we hadn't tasted water for weeks. Those cold drinks certainly tasted good. We got sort of swelled up from our greediness, but the thirst you get in the desert is wicked. Then we investigated and discovered this wasn't the base we were supposed to be at, either. Our destination was still some five miles away. So, having had a nice drink with the second lot of B-24 boys and a good meal with the first, we took our planes over to the third base, which turned out to be the right one and there we stayed for the night.

The place cooled off as soon as the sun went down, and we felt fine. We had a chance to take in an outside movie, and as entertainment was scarce and would be scarcer in China, we all decided to go. After the movie we all went to the Officers' Club and had some more lemonade. The barracks were very crowded, so we slept outside that night. As we lay in our cots under the stars we started a big argument. It was on a subject that is not unusual in any outfit where there is a boy, or maybe two, from Texas. All you have to do is make a crack about Texas, just ask, "Oh, is Texas in the Union now?" and you are really in the middle of something. That was the kind of argument we had that night in Bengasi. I don't remember who started the fireworks that time, but somehow we drifted along and all got absorbed in a hotly contested repeat performance of the Civil War. Listening to it, you might have felt that the present war was really a far-off subject. Kidding and cracking jokes, the boys one by one dropped off to sleep under the open sky. Sleeping came easy that night, for we figured we had done a good day's work.

Early the next morning we took off for Cairo. We were all looking forward to seeing the famous Egyptian town that we had heard so much about all our lives. The afternoon before, Johnny Opsvig had lost his canopy on landing, but he insisted on going on. He flew his ship in all some four thousand miles without a canopy and with the terrific wind tearing at his head all the way. It was extreme, but it was typical of the way every man in the squadron felt. Your ship would have to be grounded for sure before you would be willing to call it quits. Bengasi to Cairo wasn't too long a flight, but it was all over the desert. The heat from the white sand formed updrafts that made it a very bumpy ride. Our checkpoints today were something special in the line of checkpoints—the Nile, the Sphinx and the Pyramids. "Join the Air Force and see the World!" I hope my pals in the Navy won't mind this little crack, but we were certainly getting around and seeing things. I had seen pictures of the Pyramids and the Sphinx in my schoolbooks, of course. I also was used to seeing them pop up wherever cigarettes are sold. But now they were our checkpoints, and that seemed strange indeed. I wonder how good old Tutankhamen— or whatever his name was—feels about the matter. Maybe he just doesn't care.

I was still flying Lieutenant Helms' wing and we sailed right along. The first part of the flight was drab. Then the Nile was sighted, and we turned up its course and saw, there in the distance, the great Pyramids. Somehow it was a solemn moment. We circled around the enormous structures, and I couldn't help thinking that our slim, fast little P-38's against these huge old piles of stone must make a real contrast of ages.

We took a good look at the Sphinx and then flew around the Cairo airport getting ready to land. I had some slight difficulties in getting down. Little Butch had somehow lost her hydraulic pressure, and I couldn't get my wheels down. I had to pump them down, which takes about five hundred strokes of a hand pump. When I landed, I was pretty well done in. We found quite a reception committee on hand, for no one in that area had seen a P-38 before.

Near the operations office in Cairo, we spotted a stand selling cold soda pop. This simply looked too good to be true. It's the sort of thing you only have a right to expect back home in America. It was no mirage, though, and the man who ran the stand made plenty of shillings that day. We were covering ground so fast that we couldn't use up the money we had changed at our last stop. It was giving us some trouble, too, for we didn't know the value of all those strange coins and bills very well. A little bit of a bill that didn't look like much at all would sometimes prove to have been worth two or three dollars. Now if we had had two or three substantial looking greenbacks in our hands instead, we wouldn't have thought of giving all of them as a tip. But we were green at shillings and pounds, and those who took our tips were not so very eager to enlighten us. I know the British were sorry to see the Americans arrive because we spoiled the natives, but it was simply ignorance on our part. That money simply didn't mean a thing to us.

The first flight, led by Lieutenant Enslen, arrived ahead of us and was scheduled to leave the next morning. I was in the second flight, but we couldn't leave so soon because of my hydraulic leak. I wasn't sorry to have to spend a day or so in Cairo, for I wanted to see the place, and so did the other boys. I ran into an old friend in the operations office in Cairo, Lieutenant Johnny O'Connor, known to everybody as Oakie. With his help we planned to see the town that evening. Schultz and Moonbeam had arrived in Cairo that day too, coming all the way from Constantine, Algiera, in one hop. It was a terrific haul, but a good bed and a cooling drink were enough of an incentive to keep Moon and Schultz going all day.

Cairo was almost like an American city. We were housed in a large hotel, and we even had sheets on our beds. Sheets, by this time, had become one of those far-off dreams of home, so this was a special treat. We had dinner that night on the veranda of the hotel, and that was like home too. The bars at the hotels had beer and liquors. None of us had seen any liquor since coming to Africa. After dinner we set out with Oakie, who really knew the town. We saw night clubs and floor shows, and after laughing and having a circus at one night club we would go on to another. The second place we went to had a reputation for having delicious steaks, and that made all our mouths water, we had been living on K rations and Spam for so long. Spam had been our regular diet since arriving in Africa three months ago, and although we didn't mind it too much at first, after about one solid month of anything three times a day you somehow lose your appetite for it. The cook would bravely boil it, broil it, fry it, bake it, and try it any other way he could think of, it was still Spam. The mere rumor of a steak was enough to send us on the double.

When we arrived at the Club, we found we had to be a member or something. The boys lined up and gave various names, such as Lieutenant Slipstream, Captain Zilch, and so on, and became members. It was only for one night anyway, so it didn't make any difference. The club turned out to be a very high class outdoor restaurant with a dance floor and a fifteen piece orchestra. I thought to myself, "All this—and a steak too!" The steak was a dream, but substantial enough to convince anybody of its reality. I don't know when I have enjoyed a meal so much. Some of the boys were imbibing rather freely of the liquor, since we hadn't had any for so long. I knew that a couple of them had to fly the next day and really felt concerned about them. Later on in the trip I asked them how they had managed the next day, and several of them swore they didn't even know they were flying for hours. I think that was laying it on sort of thick, but I'd be willing to bet the motors that day weren't the only things throbbing.

At dinner we were being kidded by some civilians at the place. These men were Americans working in Cairo on construction work of some kind. It would have been okay if the kidding had been done by other members of the squadron, because that went on all the time, but it wasn't all right for some outsider to stick his nose in. The thugs were saying we were chumps to be in the army. They claimed to be making large chunks of dough while we were doing all the fighting for them. We could have cleaned up on them in no time, but the club was a nice one and there was no sense in starting a fight. It irked us more than a bit, but we tried to ignore them. They were just a bunch of drunks, anyway. Then Moonbeam hit on a brilliant idea. We played dumb, as if we were suckers through and through, and they swallowed the bait and got to acting more and more important and swanking around like anything. A little later Moon asked Schultz if he could give him some American money for three hundred French francs which he had left over from North Africa. He said that loud enough for the construction boys to hear. He knew, of course, that those French francs weren't worth more than a few bucks in our money, but he figured that the civilians didn't know. He wasn't mistaken, for when Schultz replied that he was sorry, but that he hadn't seen that much American money in a long while, they came horning in anxious to swank about how much they were making. They pulled out a mighty roll of American bills and paid Moon off a lot more than his francs were worth. They thought they were wise guys, all right, but whether they meant to or not, what they actually did was to pay for the dinners of some twenty American pilots. We may have been suckers, but we sure wound up on the long end of that transaction.

The next day, Schultz, Lieutenant Ivan Rockwell and I went out shopping. All our baggage had been shipped ahead by transport plane because there wasn't much more room in our P-38's for personal effects. However, we were all short of stuff, I in particular, and since we had a little extra room we bought what we could. We managed to get one or two items, so we felt we had accomplished something. In the afternoon, after our planes were ready, we went out to see the Sphinx and the Pyramids. They impressed us even more on second and closer view. They are so big and look so strange and mysterious. We thought they were a great and awe-inspiring sight.

It was in Cairo that we ran into the real thing in the line of beggars and street vendors. North Africa had enough of them, but they would go away and stop bothering you when you indicated you weren't interested. In Cairo, I swear those boys must have taken lessons from the original traveling salesman. They were always stationed outside our hotels because the Americans were known as easy targets. They "sold" everything from shoe-shines to sabers. Most of the boys bought swagger sticks with a bundle of horsehair tied at one end to chase away flies, but if they could have bought something to chase away the vendors themselves, I am sure they would have been willing to pay most any price for it. Schultz was the best touch those boys had seen in years. That afternoon as he walked from the hotel over to the restaurant, a distance of about fifty yards, he purchased five swagger sticks before he could manage to get away. Each vendor offered him a better price than the last and each time Schultz thought he was making a better deal. The last seller of swagger sticks probably only charged him three times what the stick was worth. Bob got razzed about that all the rest of the trip.

We were all set for the take-off the next morning at dawn, and we had made arrangements to help out our enlisted men at the field there in a little deal. The Army didn't have a real post in Cairo, and the men stationed there were on detached service. Up to that time, the British fliers had been giving them a lot of friendly razzing about their fighter planes. The British squadrons had Spitfires and Hurricanes on the field, and every morning they proceeded to get our boys out of bed by buzzing. To return this favor was right down our alley. When the P-38's had landed, their presence had boosted our boys' morale a hundred percent in the running argument about whose fighter planes were the best, and we had promised them that when we took off we would give the British boys a morning buzz that would be second to none. The British barracks were a short distance from the field and right in line with the runways. We took off in formation and circled the field. We were about two thousand feet up when we came screaming down over the barracks. If you have ever heard a P-38, you know that the plane sorta whistles. This noise doesn't hit you until the ship is past, it goes so fast. We just about took the roofs off those barracks, and the British boys started to climb out windows, doors or anything that was handy. After that, we trusted our boys would be left in peace for a while.

The flight that day was to one of our secret bases in Iraq. It was an uneventful flight, but for many of us it was even more special than our flight to Egypt and the pyramids. For today we were going to fly directly over the Holy Land. I had read about Jerusalem several thousand times in my catechism in grade school, and it seemed almost unbelievable that today I was calmly flying over it in a formation of P-38's. It was a strange and penetrating feeling that came over me as I thought that down there in the territory over which we were hurtling was the birthplace of Christ. I would have liked to stop and make a pilgrimage to Jerusalem and Nazareth. As we went over, I said a prayer, thinking that being that close to the Savior's birthplace would make it a special prayer that might be of special help to a little group of men who were soon going to look death in the face.

We landed at our base and spent the night. Early the next morning we were off again to Abadan on the Persian Gulf. So far our flight had traveled at an amazing speed, but we were due for a delay here. Because of the bad haze and dust, we were unable to take off for about five days. The delay made the boys restless. Moonbeam and the last flight caught up with us here, and we were all anxious to move on. This brief spell of waiting gave me a chance to write more letters. The boys sometimes razzed me about my letter-writing, but I was a firm believer in the principle that you have to write letters in order to receive them. When the returns came in, I always had the last laugh.

Our next stop was a British base at Bahrein Island in the Persian Gulf. It was a desolate place, and hotter than blue blazes. As we moved along from base to base, we created a sensation at every stop, for nobody in this area had seen a P-38 before. It was grand to get such a reception the first time, but after a while it palled, for we were still taking care of our planes as well as flying them and had a lot of work to do. So far the ships were holding up swell. We were eagerly awaiting the meeting with our crew chiefs, though, for every ship could stand some work done on her and those boys really had the know-how for it. After another slight delay, we flew on to a small English base just inside the borders of India, just beyond Iran, on the Arabian Sea. We stopped there to refuel in order to go on to Karachi.

When I started my engines that day, a fuse blew out and I was delayed fixing my trouble. That meant I had to wait at this little base until Moon arrived. I had a very enjoyable three days there with four other officers, none of whom was an American. The Commandant was an Australian Captain who was a Flying Officer. There were also a small, peppery R.A.F. officer and two Indian officers in the weather service. These three were lieutenants but you called them left-enant, of course. We had a great time together.

The Captain was a great scout and talked very English. When he was talking about something bad, the word for it was "bloody." When it was good, it was "wizard." The Captain made it quite clear to me that he would have liked to have me stay there for good. That wasn't intended in any way as a personal compliment. It didn't matter whether I was "bloody" or not, what mattered was that he thought the P-38 was "wizard." He fell in love with Little Butch. He would have liked to fly her, and had I felt a little less anxious to make our final destination, or a little more casual about things of that sort, I would certainly have let him have his wish. But I had nursed Little Butch for many thousands of miles now, and it was too close to our destination to take any chances on something going wrong. Moonbeam and Schultz arrived and were anxious to get on to Karachi and get a drink. We slept well that night and started for Karachi the following morning. We knew it was one of the best bases we had.

With Moonbeam leading the flight through clouds, we went on to Karachi. We flew most of the way behind a large Army transport, because the big ship had a navigator, and some navigation was needed in the haze and dust that made visibility so poor.

On our arrival at Karachi, we found that our group had lost another one of its ships. Number one had been Lieutenant Rockwell's plane which had gone to pieces back in Iraq when Rocky had an engine cut on the take-off and had to belly-land. Rocky himself got away without a scratch and was now coming along by transport.

In Karachi, Lieutenant Lee Gregg, one of the best pilots in our group, lost his ship. He had turned it into the depot for a check, and the next morning when a crew chief was tuning the ship up, the power of the ship made it jump its wheel blocks and it ran through a shed. The mishap ruined one engine and necessitated an engine change. That meant we had lost two planes, but both pilots were safe and still with us. It was wonderful luck.

While we were in Karachi, we heard rumors that our first flight had reached China and had already accounted for some Zeros, the number running anywhere from three to a dozen depending on who told you. That news made us feel good; we were delighted to think that our first gang had already got into some scraps, and we were all the more anxious to get there and join them.

Karachi was one of the better towns in India, and we enjoyed our two-day stay there. Bill Bolton and Earl Helms had found a place downtown where you could get hamburgers and malted milks, and it was a greater find than gold in the streets. These good old American delicacies were really what made our stay in Karachi memorable. It was about here that some of the boys began to get sick with dysentery, which is very bad in India. Practically every newcomer joins the club, sooner or later. I was no exception—in fact, I was a charter member. It is a highly inconvenient disease to have if you have to fly five hour hops cramped into the small cockpit of a P-38. But we were all determined to get to China as quickly as we could, dysentery or not.

We flew on to Agra, where we finally met up with our crew chiefs. It was a glorious reunion, and Little Butch seemed to smile joyfully when she saw Technical Sergeant Shaffer. Sergeant Shaffer was a quiet boy who had been all through the North African campaign. He could work like a trojan. What he didn't know about a P-38 you could put on the point of a pin. It was his work that kept Little Butch up there in the sky at all times. While the crew chiefs gave the ships the hundred-hour inspection, we took it easy at the base at Agra. The mess at the post was the finest I have ever eaten at overseas. I think the cook must have had influential friends, for he managed to produce meals made up of the most delicious food imaginable. Where he ever got the makings that went into his masterpieces I couldn't imagine. My inconvenient disease was still with me, but it didn't seem to affect my appetite, nor the appetites of any of my fellow sufferers.

When the ships were ready, we took off for Gaya. It was only an overnight stop, and from there we went on to Chabua. This was our base at the foot of the mighty Himalayas.

I had had a grand time flying through India. All the way I had been flying the wing of Lieutenant Bob Barrett. Bob was the high man of the squadron, having knocked down four jerries in battle. We had decided that we would stick together to China, if possible, and Captain Palmer okayed the project. All across India, we followed the big transport. He was holding a straight course at about 170 miles per hour. We could practically do circles and spirals around him at our speed of about 240 m.p.h. It gave us good practice in formation flying though. And so far as I was concerned, I knew I would be pleased to have Bob Barrett head my flight any day of the year.

At Chabua we were again held up because of bad weather. Getting over the worst mountain range in the world called for almost perfect weather. We couldn't fly our ships on instruments over such dangerous terrain. They were too speedy and often would be about five hundred feet ahead of any instruments devised. So there was nothing we could do but wait, and wait we did.

While we were at Chabua we had a piece of bad news. It wasn't really tragic, but it struck us right between the eyes just the same. Our baggage had all been lost. The transport it was on got across the Hump all right, but then it developed trouble and crashed. The crew all bailed out safely, but our baggage didn't know how to bail out and went to a fiery end with the plane. This was the second time within six months that I had lost everything I owned, and I resolved that I wouldn't buy another uniform until I got home to the States. It really wasn't very funny to lose all those new duds, painfully got together since I had come to Africa. Much of it I had just purchased in Karachi. It was a consolation though that I had lots of company in my misery. There were some twenty odd pilots all in the same boat.

In Chabua too we met Colonel Bruce Holloway. He had been sent over from China to lead us the rest of the way. We had not heard of him before, but judging from his actions and general bearing we could guess, we thought, that he must have a desk job somewhere as a regular thing. General Chennault must want us pretty badly, we figured, to send such a lot of rank over to get us. During the days we were waiting around, Colonel Holloway told us about the Japs. He had been in China with the first American gang and was now the commanding officer of the 23rd Fighter Group, formerly the "Flying Tigers." He had flown the P-38 for only one hour and was a regular P-40 pilot. It was interesting to hear him talk about the missions. But it wasn't until some time later that we ran into a lieutenant on his way home who told us that Colonel Holloway was the leading Ace in this whole theater. He had eleven ships at this time, and increased that score considerably before he left. He used to fly around to various advance bases hoping there would be a good fight while he was there. If he was at the wrong base, and another one got the fight, he was sore as a boil. The General often objected to his going out on so many missions, but apparently he was a real flying fool who wanted to wage war behind the guns of a fighter plane and not from behind a desk. We were certainly mistaken in our first impression of this mild-mannered, calm acting man. In the months that were to follow, we were to get much better acquainted with him, and every man in the squadron respected him as a great guy and a great flier.

We took off on a sunny day to try to get over the Hump. The weather report had carried word that the weather had broken at Kunming, our destination. We climbed rapidly to a high altitude trying to sail over the high range. We got to 32,000 feet and still couldn't top that high stuff the mountains threw up. We were dodging around clouds in formation when we flew into a pocket. The only opening was the one through which we had come in. Colonel Holloway called for a 180 degree turn to the left. I was flying the Colonel's wing and went around. I guess not everyone had heard him, because airplanes were going all over. Bob Barrett had taken over Moon's place as cleanup man. In the wild scramble, Bob had taken to the overcast to keep from hitting one of the other men. His ship went into a spin and he called over the radio, "Moonbeam, where are you?" He said his ship was in a spin, and then that he had it out again but was in the overcast and wanted to know our position. Moon called back, "We are at 30,000 feet heading 220 degrees, fly this heading for forty minutes and then pick up 235 degrees and you will come out in the valley." Bob replied that he understood and would follow instructions. "Okay," he radioed, "I'll see you back at the field." That was the last we saw or heard from Bob Barrett. It was about two months later that a search party found his plane on the side of a mountain. He had apparently tried to let down through the overcast, and smacked right into something solid up there.

Bob's loss was the first in our new squadron, and it was taken very hard. I felt particularly bad, for he was my special buddy and we had planned to fly together. We kept up hope for about three weeks, always thinking in the back of our minds that maybe some day ole Bob would come walking in from the hills. It was a bitter pill to have to give up hope for him, but we resolved to try twice as hard and get a few extra Japs for his sake. If he had had the chance he would have accounted for some of them, but oftentimes the enemy isn't the toughest opponent a flier has to face.

After this first attempt to break over, in which Bob Barrett was lost, we returned to Chabua and waited for another break in the weather. The break came, and we took to the air again to tangle with the Hump. This time we made it, and we went all the way through to Kunming. Flying over the towering Himalayas that day was one of the most beautiful and awe-inspiring experiences of my life. I shuddered, though, when I thought of those gallant boys who fly across that Hump twice a day whatever the weather, fair or foul. I had to cross the Hump five times in all, and if I never have to do it again it won't make me mad.

After we got across the mountains, China looked like a make-believe land for sure. Everything was green, and the countryside smelled fresh. The rains had kept the air clean for the time being. When we landed, I was very much impressed with what I saw. There seemed to be millions of coolies toiling everywhere. Their methods were primitive, but the results they got were not.

After long weeks of work and worry we had arrived at our destination at last. Out of the twenty-five planes we had started with, we had arrived with twenty-two, a good record for such a difficult flight. We hoped that it wouldn't be long now before we got into the real scrap. And that hope was to be fulfilled.

THE OPENING DOG FIGHT

10

"GENERAL CHENNAULT WANTS YOU to report to his office at once." That was the message. We had just landed at the field and were getting out of our planes when a messenger hurried around to each one of us.

We were overwhelmed at the idea of a personal interview with General Chennault. Later on we found out that we were not exceptional characters, but that a talk with the General was always the first thing on the schedule when you entered under his command.

I walked over to Schultz's plane and togther we climbed into a jeep for the ride over to headquarters. It was an exciting moment. We had all read and heard a million stories about General Claire L. Chennault. He was practically a legendary figure to us. His "Flying Tigers" had made air history, and their exploits in the air over China loomed big in our mnds. We had heard that the Japs had estimated Chennault's air force to be between four and five hundred planes in those days, for it had such a tremendous hitting power; actually, at that time the General was operating with some thirty-five or forty obsolete P-40's. Those had been the pioneer days of air combat in China.

It was with deep respect and some awe that Schultz and I and all the other boys went through the door of headquarters. We entered the General's office and were told to sit down. The General began to talk to us about the Japs and their tactics, and we made a great effort to keep our minds tight on what he was saying. The moment of meeting our General should have been a solemn occasion, but there was another factor that made it difficult for us to keep up the right serious attitude. In the same room with us sat the General's secretary. She was a very attractive girl. As if magnetized, the glances of about twenty fighter pilots were going in her direction while the General was explaining the method which the men of his group had found best in fighting the Japs. The pilots of our group were making every effort to grasp what he said and look at Miss Davis at the same time. It really made a funny picture—even funnier than the cartoons you see of some male comedian trying to entertain the boys and sweating blood in the effort while their attention is riveted on the pretty girl who stands at the side of the stage and does nothing. In our case, the boys had just completed a long, tough flight of thousands of miles, and in all the time they had been overseas they had almost no opportunity to see a good-looking American girl. Now they had that opportunity and did they seize it! This gazing went on for some time, until General Chennault broke down and laughed. I am sure he had been aware of what was happening all along, and we began to understand why his men called him "Pappy" Chennault.

During that conference we did learn something about the Japs in spite of the big distraction we were subjected to. Before we had finished, General Chennault had told us what our purpose in the 14th Air Force would be. His personal talk made a great impression on all of us. We felt we were learning first hand from the one man who knew the Japs like a book, and we drank in his words. We were to be officially designated as the 449th Fighter Squadron, attached temporarily to the 23rd Fighter Group, that is, to the "Flying Tigers." The record that we had to shoot at was certainly a great one and nothing could possibly have offered a greater incentive to us. I know that in our hearts was one great resolve—to try to be the best Fighter Squadron in all China. We left General Chennault's office with that resolve in our minds, all hoping for a quick crack at real action. We didn't have long to wait.

After the conference with the General, we were driven up to one of the "Hostels," as the barracks in China are known. Night had come, and as we drove into the hostel area we saw that it was more or less deserted. The entire group of boys who lived there were crowded into the mess hall viewing a movie. We were assigned rooms, and began to notice that the evening was quite cool. Talking to a couple of the enlisted men who had just come over from the field, we learned that, due to the elevation of this part of the country, the temperature seldom soared. Schultz and I went inside and sat around our room talking about anything and everything. We were interrupted in this general conversation by Moonbeam, who came in to tell us that we had a mission scheduled for tomorrow morning at dawn. The news sent a thrill down my spine, but it didn't last long. I heard the extra piece of news that I had been elected to take the enlisted men up to our permanent base by transport plane. Little Butch was to be flown on the mission by Major Ed Goss. Major Goss was a veteran of the warfare in China and a crack pilot, so I didn't worry about Little Butch being in his hands, although I sort of hated to have anybody else fly

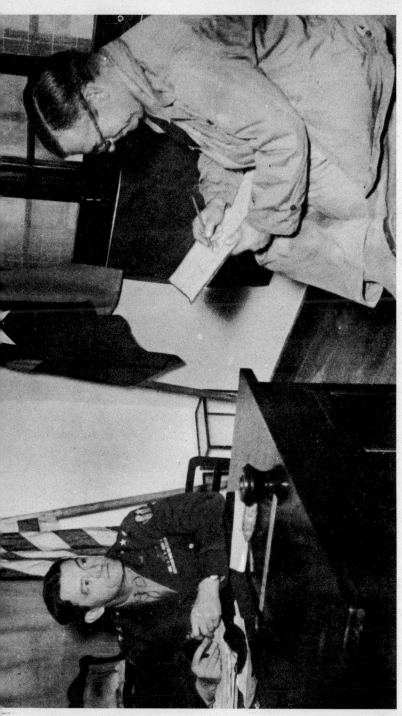

Caricature artist Don Barclay sketches Major General Clair L. Chennault, commanding general of the 14th Air Force.

her. The Major was the commanding officer of a Fighter Squadron and had seven victories to his credit. General Chennault had delegated him to lead our squadron for three weeks. After that Captain Palmer would be ready to take over.

We were soon to find out that flying in China is not easy. The territory is almost the world's worst as far as navigation is concerned, for from the air every Chinese village looks like every other, and there are few landmarks to help the poor pilot or navigator.

The next morning at dawn, my heart skipped a couple of beats when the boys took off on their mission. The briefing had been that the boys were to tackle a Jap airfield on their way to our permanent base. Schultz gave me the razz as he left that morning, and I certainly wished I could have gone along. After they left, Lieutenant Machado and I gathered all the enlisted men and supplies and started out. Our permanent base was about 750 miles from the 14th Air Force Headquarters. It wasn't going to be a fast ride in the transport, and the thought of the boys on their first mission made it sort of an uneasy ride.

It took us hours to arrive at our base. From above we could hardly make out the field, so well was it blended into the surrounding territory. On the field we could see the outlines of a lot of planes, which we found on landing were dummies of P-40's. Stacked in a neat row were the P-38's. We counted the ships automatically and were relieved to know that everybody had arrived safely.

I was eager to hear about the mission from Schultz, and went in search of him as soon as I could. There was no news, though, for the mission had been changed and they had flown directly to the new base. I hadn't missed anything after all.

We drove up to our new Hostels and looked the place over. To us it looked like heaven. We had very nice rooms and beds with sheets on them. Africa had never been like this! Schultz, Moon and I took one of the rooms. This was to be some combination, three of the squadron's craziest loons in the same room. Everybody drew rooms and settled in. It made us feel as though we had actually arrived at the scene of serious operations, to be at our permanent base. It had been some time since we had settled down in any room with the expectation of sticking with it more than a couple of days.

The best part of the whole deal was that we were now alone, on our own. We didn't have any headquarters around that we would have to be going to all the time. We depended on each other entirely. The

449th was a flying squadron, and at the time of our arrival there were few men in the ground personnel. There was Lieutenant Hutter who took charge of the personnel and Lieutenant Allen in charge of the radio department. These two and Captain Mohr, the Armaments Officer, who had remained in Kunming, were the only non-flying officers in the squadron at the start. Later on we got a couple of fine Irishmen, Lieutenant Murphy for Supply and Lieutenant Monaghan for Armament. The rest of the jobs were handled by flying officers who doubled up on their jobs. Schultz was made Engineering Officer, Moon Operations Officer, Helms was the Mess Officer, Machado the Motor Pool Officer, and I was handed the job of Special Service Officer. These duties were in addition to our flying, which of course came first.

Everyone pitched right in to work for the squadron. At that time we were to fly only interception missions and were anxiously waiting for the Japs to come in.

When we had arrived at the base, we had rejoined five officers, Lieutenants Enslen, Helms, Bolton, Beardsley and Longueil, who had come in the first flight considerably ahead of us. They had already seen action, as we had heard when we were still back in India. Enslen and Helms each had a Zero to his credit and the outfit was doing okay.

Captain Palmer and Moon got busy at once making up the schedule of the flights. Major Goss was still leading us and doing a super job. Flight leaders were selected, and it was Moon for the first flight, Bill Bolton for flight two, and Lowden Enslen for flight three. These were the men who would lead us against the Japs, and not one of us doubted their ability to do it.

Bill Bolton, or William Bolton as his official papers listed him, was the lead man in the squadron as far as experience was concerned. He had flown forty-eight missions in Africa, and had volunteered to come to China. He would have needed only two more missions in Africa to be eligible to go home for a furlough, but he elected action in China instead. Bolt was as steady as any man in the outfit, and that included some pretty cool cucumbers. He had had several victories in África, and he was also known for his ability to train the more inexperienced pilots and make veterans out of them in no time. His wingmen always came back.

Lieutenant Lowden Enslen probably had the highest amount of flying time in a P-38 to his credit. He had chalked up about 800 hours, which is a lot of time in the air in any plane. Ens had been ferrying the P-38 between England and Africa with Schultz, and he had flown several missions over Italy and North Africa. He was a wonderful navigator. His navigation never missed. He could hit a pin point on a map, and in China that is a real accomplishment.

The third flight leader was ole Moonbeam. Words just can't do justice to that crazy redhead. He had the toughest job in the bunch, for the Operations Officer is bound to be the most "cussed out" man in any squadron. He had to try to satisfy a whole gang of pilots all of whom were "eager," and all of whom wanted to fly every mission. It was a stiff job, and he did it up brown. In the air he never made a mistake. He had had a couple of close calls in the air over Africa, and had become what the Air Force boys term a "Christian," or a safe and seasoned flier, having become convinced in Africa that "head up and locked" stunts only make the neck shorter and serve no other purpose.

Our first days at the base were filled with anxiety for action. We were raring to go but we still had a good many things to learn.

General Chennault had told us about his warning system, which he had devised as soon as he came to China as head of the Chinese Air Force. He had asked the help and cooperation of every man, woman and child in China. He got that cooperation, too. The network warning of the approach of Japanese planes covers the country, and the American forces are generally notified two or three hours before the Japs arrive. The network functions for Chungking, the capital, and it also functions for all the individual airfields all over the country. It seems that every Chinese, wherever he may be, is constantly on the lookout for enemy planes, and as soon as he spots them or hears their motors, he gets word somehow to a main switchboard. I don't know how they do it, whether they wig-wag, or have some other system—certainly they can't have telephones everywhere out in the vast Chinese countryside. But the fact remains that the target area is warned. The Japs have to fly over long stretches of inhabited country, and they cannot fail to be observed. As the information comes in from the watchers, the mile by mile course of the Japs is plotted on a large map. The entire system is handled by the Chinese, and has been of inestimable value to us. It has one special feature that has saved the lives of a good many American fliers. If a pilot gets lost, all he has to do is go to the nearest town and circle it. The Chinese then report him as over such and such a town, and the American Radio Operations flash him instructions as to what course to take to get back to his field. Surely it takes a loyal and courageous people to work a complicated system like that. And the Chinese are such a people.

The 449th pilots at the alert shack: Lieutenants Longueil, Rea, Gregg, Weber, Dowis, and Captain Enslen.

In our early days at the alert shack, everyone would jump when the first plot would go on the board. If we had had our way, we would have been up in the air right away doing nothing but waste a lot of precious gasoline. Major Goss, however, with his experience in that theater, would sit still and calmly follow the course of the enemy planes. He wasn't going to have us up in the air for nothing, not he, for he knew that gasoline is more precious than gold in China, and what we had we had to make count. When the Japs did get close enough, Major Goss would say, "Okay, they are coming in. Let's get 'em." The men would run to their ships and take off. The procedure was standard, and went on every day. It is undoubtedly still going on every day all over free China.

The boys in our squadron were terribly anxious to hop on some Japs, and after six alerts we still had not contacted them. On these warm evenings, before we went to bed, we used to sit on the porches of our hostels and hope that tomorrow would be the day. We had more pilots than planes, and the schedule was usually worked out so that you flew three days and then were off one. The men who were not scheduled to go up hoped that no Japs would come around until the next day. It was always the same story, everyone wanted to be up there to greet them when they did arrive. The 449th may not have succeeded in its resolve to be the best squadron in China, but by the time the Japs got there it was certainly the most ambitious.

About one week passed, but although we had been in the air on several occasions we had not made contact with the enemy. Then one day the telephone rang once again; the Chinese soldier on duty picked it up; he listened for a minute, then put the first plot on the board. The men sat watching the Japs' progress. Every one of them seemed to be saying silently, "Come on in, you little sons-of-nippon, we'll be waiting for you!" The moment came, the boys ran to their planes, and they were all hoping as they ran that this would be the day.

It was the day. The Zeros were flying at 30,000 feet when we spotted them coming right head-on. Schultz was flying on Major Goss's wing, and off they went into the leaders. Bill Bolton took his flight into the left of the Zeros, and Sam Palmer went to the right with the other flight. Major Goss cut loose and a Zero went down smoking. Schultz pressed the gun teat and another Zero that had been trying to get Major Goss went down in smoke. Bill Bolton made a head-on run with an element of Zeros and sent one down. The rest of the Zeros dove toward earth and went for home. We P-38's had been instructed to stay at altitude, because the P-40's from a nearby base were also in the fray and would hop on the Zeroes if they went down. That was all of the first battle for the 449th.

When our boys landed, they doped out that a pretty good day's work had been done. The P-38's claimed three probables and the P-40's claimed two. The reason the P-38's only claimed probables was that they were following the fighters' code of claiming a kill as sure only when one of three things has happened. The pilot himself or another pilot on the same mission must see the enemy ship explode or catch fire. Or else he must see the pilot bail out, or the actual crash of the ship on the ground. For one of these three reasons alone can a pilot confirm his victories. Our boys were at 30,000 feet that afternoon and they couldn't follow a damaged Jap plane down because their orders were to keep that altitude. No one saw any of the three events required in order to claim a victory, and therefore only "probables" could be claimed at that time.

The next day the ground men located the five Jap Zeros on the ground. The three probables claimed by the P-38's and the two claimed by the P-40's were then confirmed in good order.

I think I felt as excited as Schultz did that night after he had got his first Jap, and Schultz certainly felt like a million. Moon wasn't on the flight, and you could have heard his yells of protest clear over in India. The Moonbeam wanted a crack at the Zeros so badly, you could see he was almost tasting it. We all felt that the 449th was off to a swell start, though the men who were not flying that day were fit to be tied because they had yet to see the Zeros. The time wasn't far away, though, when everybody in the outfit would have seen their Zeros, and plenty of them.

The evening after the first scrap we had a meeting to talk over the day's work. There had been a few small flaws in the flying, and it was agreed that we would meet every night in order to thrash out any difficulties. Major Goss had seen a lot of fighting in the China theater, and he said the boys had done a swell job of it, so we were happy although not altogether satisfied with ourselves.

After the meeting Moonbeam and I cornered Schultz and asked him what the dope on the Zero was. Bob said he hadn't had much of a chance to make observations, but he thought he had noticed that when a Zero tried to turn with a P-38 at that altitude, the ship spun out of the turn. That would have been a good point to know if it had been true. We were eager to find out more about it. We had been instructed by General Chennault under no condition to try to turn with a Zero. The ship was so light that it could turn inside any of our ships. However, maybe the P-38 was different, and if so this new piece of information might mean a real advantage for our gang. That was what we were looking for. Our tactics were to fight the Japs where he didn't want to fight. That was the General's secret with the P-40. The ship had tremendous diving power and good firepower, and the P-40 pilots used these two advantages on the Japs and lived to enjoy their victories. We knew that we had a better ship than the P-40, but it would take a good deal of time and practice to better their record. They had about a twelve to one score over the Japs, and that was good shooting in any man's league.

When we first came to China, we knew that a great deal was expected of us. Everybody had heard about what a great ship the P-38 was, and we were expected to set the world on fire with it. That was okay with us, too, for that was what we wanted to do, but we needed time to prove to everybody that we wouldn't let them down. We were the only P-38's in China, all other fighters were P-40's. I have often said the greatness of those P-40's in China was not in the machine; it was in the men that General Chennault had flying them. These men were the finest pilots in the world. They took on the Zeros, a type of ship that was superior to theirs in almost all respects, and whipped them badly.

Of course, a first class machine will always arouse the envy of a first class pilot, and I don't think I was mistaken if I felt during our early days in China an air of tension surrounding us because we were flying P-38's. However, as the days went on and we all flew together helping each other out wherever we could, that feeling disappeared and a warm welcome greeted us and our P-38's every time we landed at one of the P-40 bases.

I don't think it could be said too often: those P-40 boys were simply great. We would have a long way to go before we could beat their record, but you couldn't keep an outfit from trying! In the months that followed we came to know men like Major Richardson, Major Costello and the rest of the P-40 boys. We knew what they had done and what they were doing. So far as we were concerned, the P-40 boys could fly on our team any time. That didn't mean that we stopped kidding them about their "broken-down junkheap," or that they weren't ready any time to come right back with plenty of cracks about the P-38. But it did mean that all of us, the P-38's as well as the

Captain Cline, Major Richardson, Harmon, and Captain Spitzer. Richardson, one of China's aces, commands a fighter squadron.

P-40's, felt keenly that we were in this together, a sort of All-American team, sticking together one for all and all for one, whether we happened to be flying washboards or the most recent model fresh off the assembly line back in the good ole U.S.A.

The boys now were getting more experienced every day in every way. During the next month we were out practicing skip-bombing every morning. We were in for something big. We knew that the P-38 was a perfect dive-bomber. It had earned this reputation because of the counter-rotating propellers. This prevented the ship from having any torque, and for dive-bombing this is an essential feature.

Skip-bombing is fun, but it isn't very healthy. The same holds for strafing a target on the ground. Flak, and small arms fire if handled correctly, can make mince-meat of you in nothing flat if they ever catch up with you. In both skip-bombing and strafing, we were depending upon our tremendous speed and the element of surprise. We had the speed, and if we achieved surprise we could raise a little general hell with the Jap ships.

During those first weeks we suffered our first loss in action. We went out on a skip-bombing mission one day. The mission was successful and we thought we had done plenty of damage to those babes down on the ground, but Rocky Rockwell had his right engine shot out in the attack. He was coming home on his left engine which was still good. We were within about ten miles of one of our bases when it heated up on him. Rocky called Lee Gregg, who was flying with him, and said, "This baby is getting too hot, Lee, I'm going to leave it."

Gregg told him to go ahead and that he would follow him down to see that he got there okay. Rocky then let go of his safety belt and tried to jettison his canopy. For some unknown reason the canopy didn't come off, but slammed back and knocked Rocky on the head He went down with the ship from about five thousand feet. Gregg saw the whole thing happen.

Everybody in the squadron felt Rocky's loss very much, for he was one of the best-liked boys in our gang and one of the finest pilots. His loss brought our casualties up to two.

A third loss followed soon after. We had two boys in the squadron whose names were almost alike, Enslen and Enssler. They pronounced their names almost the same, and we called them "double S" or "single S" when we wanted to make a distinction. George Enssler was nineteen years old, the youngest boy in the oufit, but one of the best. He got into a big fight in a dive-bombing mission over Hankow and lost one of his engines. He couldn't make it back to our base. His ship was on fire, and he himself was wounded by some of the flak that had got his engine. He made a belly landing in his flaming plane and got out of it alive, but he died a short time later of his wounds and the burns he had received before he could get his ship down. He was a mighty brave kid.

So Rocky Rockwell and George Enssler had left the 449th to join the flight of Bob Barrett. We swore revenge on the Japs for their loss, and as the months rolled by we got it.

The P-40 squadrons had been in China for over a year and had established a great list of victories. We hoped that by the time we had been on the scene that long, the 449th would have at least as good a score as those crack veterans. The real excitement was yet to come for our squadron, but we were keeping plenty busy and were ready for whatever came our way.

THE ENEMY—THE JAP AND THE ZERO

11

WE WERE ABOUT 750 miles from the nearest good town at our Chinese base, and by good town I mean a town where you can get a decent steak dinner. But from the point of view of flying, which was what mattered, our position was very central. From our base, we could cover all the P-40 bases in the area every time they had a raid. The Japs hit the P-40 bases a lot more than they ever tried to hit us. In fact, they only raided our base once in eight months.

We didn't know why it was that the Japs stayed away from us with so much care. Possibly they didn't think the 38's were important enough to bother with, but we didn't think that was very likely. We much preferred to believe that the 38's were something the Japs didn't want to face if they didn't have to, and I think we were quite right in that. At any rate, they showed a pronounced preference for targets where they might have a chance of getting in and running out again before the 38's had a chance to catch up. The P-38 has a lot of firepower in her nose. I know I would hate to make a head-on pass against four 50-caliber machine guns and one 20 mm. cannon, and very likely the Japs felt the same way about it.

We knew from experience that the Japs seldom made a head-on pass at us in the air, and several times the Zeros scattered and ran when the P-38's turned into them.

The one head-on encounter I saw was between Lee Gregg and a Zero in a fight over Heng Yang. Gregg had more nerve and plain guts than any other man I had ever known, and no mission was dangerous enough to suit him. Up there high over Heng Yang, Gregg and a Zero squared away head-on. Gregg was hitting the Zero with his bullets, but couldn't seem to slam one in a vital spot. He and the Jap pilot flew right straight at each other, both shooting everything they could, and that was plenty. Gregg refused to budge from his course and was determined to fly right through the Jap if necessary. At very short range, just before the two planes would have been in actual collision, one of Gregg's bullets hit home and the Zero exploded. The Jap had succeeded in knocking out Gregg's right engine during the last second before he went down. Gregg just turned over on his back and went home on one engine. His average speed on the trip back was about 210 miles per hour on his one engine, which isn't exactly standing still.

From our base in the central part of the net the P-38's soared up to the assistance of any P-40 base under attack. We were able to get up to a high altitude and knock them down for the 40's to polish off, and that system worked out very well. Before the P-38's arrived in China, the Japs always had the advantage of a higher ceiling, for the P-40 is not a high altitude fighter. And in a dog-fight, the man who has the higher altitude on the first pass had an advantage that is hard to beat. I can well imagine the surprised look on the Japs' faces the day they first looked above them and found the P-38's screaming down for the kill. Before that time, they never had to worry about anything being above them.

Every time we tangled with the Japs we learned something more about them. After every fight, the squadron held a business meeting to go over the experiences of the day, and the information we exchanged in that way was of great benefit to everybody.

Due to the difficulty in getting supplies into China, the American forces there have so far always been outnumbered by the Japs, but they have set the most amazing record in the war in the low ratio of their own losses as compared with those of the enemy. I don't know what the ratio is for all the squadrons in China, but for the 449th it was eleven Jap ships destroyed for every one of ours lost in combat. Ours was a good record, but nothing to what some of the other squadrons had. As a matter of fact, the loss of eleven ships probably hurt the Japs less than the loss of one of ours, due to that problem of supply.

The great transports that flew daily over the Hump from India braved the most terrifying weather conditions and dangers to bring in the supplies we needed, and the fact that we never got enough of the precious stuff, that we always kept clamoring tor more, can in no way belittle the greatness and importance of what those boys of the India-China service did for the cause of the United Nations. I would rather fly a combat mission any time than tangle with that flight over the Himalayas. And yet, to see the casual way they do it, you would almost believe that to the pilots who fly those transports it is nothing more than a milk run. Many brave American boys have lost their lives over those dreadful mountain ranges, but the service still carries on day in and day out. These boys are certainly the unsung heroes of the China war, and they deserve every bit of credit that can be given them.

The Jap pilot is a dangerous foe, and we were not making any mistake about that. We had heard all about him before we tangled with him in the sky, and our experience confirmed what we had heard. However, the Japs do have several faults as fliers, and the Americans capitalize greatly on these. If I were asked the one prime reason that American pilots beat the Japs in the air, I think it would be the Japs' inability to think for themselves in a tight spot. It is just the opposite with the Americans. When the going gets tough and the chips are down, the American boy shows himself at his best. He pulls every trick he ever learned and a few that are not in the book. When the Japs fight together, they are a hard opponent. Split them up, and half the battle is won. Our tactics were always to try to bust them up so that we could get at them one at a time.

In every skill that can be acquired by sheer drill and training the Japs are A1. They certainly are the world's best formation pilots. They must be trained in formation flying until they can practically do it in their sleep. In a raid over one of our bases I saw P-40's streak in to cut Jap bombers out of formation one by one. As if they worked by machine, the next man in the formation moved in automatically to take the place of the ship that had just been shot down. Whenever they came on a bombing mission, their formation was perfection itself, but we didn't stand around and admire it. Another point I must mention at this juncture is the matter of accuracy in bombing. The Japs may have a lot of faults, but inability to hit a target is not one of them. There may be quite a lot of difference of opinion on this subject, and all I know is what I saw, but the Jap bombing raids on our fields seemed to hit what they set out to hit or at least to get uncomfortably close to it.

It was always easy to identify the approach of Jap bombers by the sound of their motors. The Japs don't synchronize the motors on their twin engined ships, and one ship gives the effect of a two ship formation, because the motors on the one ship are not set at a definite speed. So when the sound of a lot of single motors is heard, with no two in tune, everyone in the vicinity hits for the slit trenches and starts saying his prayers.

There have been a good many discussions in our mess about the merits of the Jap pilot as a gunner. I am inclined to agree with the side that thinks the Japs as fighter pilots have not mastered the art of aerial gunnery. I think this is due to two things. First, the Japs don't seem to have the imagination to adjust their gunnery to the free movements of a live target, whereas every American boy has had some experience skeet shooting and hunting, and has learned that leading a target is the main thing in shooting at a moving object. Second, the Japs do not have the armament or the fire power to match ours. Our armament is definitely superior, and a pilot who does not feel that his guns are to all intents and purposes his life line won't last long in combat. Our Army Ordnance has designed guns and bullets with a far greater firepower than anything the Japs have got, and we can stay out of range of the Japs and still hit him with our guns. This is as great an advantage in the air as it is, for example, in a naval engagement.

And then, the ground crew men that the 449th had for armament were crackerjacks at their job. One of them was "Big" Smitty. We had given him that name because we had to distinguish him from another fellow by the same name whom he called "Little" Smitty. Big Smitty was head of the armament squad for the enlisted men and worked under Lieutenant Tom Monaghan. What Big Smitty didn't know about guns just wasn't worth knowing. As for Tom Monaghan, he was as serious about his job as though he were flying the planes himself. And those two men were only two out of all the armorers in the squadron, but their feelings and ability were typical of the lot. They all knew that on their work a pilot's life and the life of his plane depended, and they never missed. We had the benefit of the best crews possible working on our equipment.

The most important point is, of course, that the American pilot, due to his general sporting training, is simply a better shot with anything than the Jap could ever hope to be. I guess the fanatical little boys never took time off to go hunting while they were building up their scheme of world conquest, and that was a serious mistake. I don't mean to imply that the Japs haven't succeeded in shooting down some of our planes, for they have and will continue to do so. Some of their pilots have shown real ability to shoot, and at times their sheer numerical superiority has counted in getting one of our planes. But the fact remains that the great majority of them can't seem to shoot for sour apples.

I have heard people say that the Japs' bad eyesight hinders their shooting. I don't believe that the slant of a guy's eyes has anything to do with how well he can shoot, for I have known enough Chinese boys who flew with us to know that that doesn't matter. Those Chinese fliers could aim and shoot with the best, as several Zeros discovered to their discomfort. In my experience of Japanese shooting, when it was bad it was always because they aimed at where the plane was at that moment, not where it was going to be by the time a shot could reach it. This peculiarity of Japanese shooting was easy to take advantage of. You just tried by all sorts of maneuvers to prevent the Jap from getting astern of you and from flying at your own level, and the chances were his shot wouldn't hit.

The Zero itself is a very fine fighter plane. The original Zero was a steal, of course, and you could practically see where each of its parts came from in design. You could often see where the material came from, too, as in the case of the soldier in Pearl Harbor who picked up a piece of Zero that had been shot down and found, stamped in plain words on the piece of aluminum, "American Aluminum Company." However, the Jap has improved the Zero very much from the original model. The Japs believe that maneuverability in a plane is the main feature to be desired, and in order to gain it they are willing to sacrifice other features, such as armored protection for the pilot and heaviness of armament in general.

After watching the Zero in action for a while, you just have to admit that it is an impressive job. But of the fighter planes lined up against us, I still don't believe it is as good as the German Messerschmitt 109, although for maneuverability it will tie the Me-109 in a knot any day.

On one occasion I saw Zeros do hammerhead stalls not more than five hundred feet above the ground, come down shooting, and get out. The wing of a Zero must pick up its air flow very fast, I guess, because if you tried that same stunt in an American plane, they would be digging you out of the ground.

Because the Zeros can zoom so low, men with any experience in China don't like to be anywhere near a guy in a foxhole shooting at the Zeros with a light machine gun. The chance of a man on the ground getting in the line of fire is too great. We had that happen to us one day. Some Chinese soldiers kept following us around with a machine gun, and we kept moving to another fox-hole to get out of their way, but they kept tagging along. It wasn't a bit comfortable. Ground fire can be very effective against a plane flying low, but the diving plane has a better chance of wiping out the ground gun and cleaning it out than the machine gun has of getting the plane. The Zero can clean out a gun position as easy as pie.

Flying against the Zeros our first rule was never to try and turn with them. That observation Schultz had made on his first flight against the Zeros, when he shot one down that seemed to start spinning in the turns, had made us hope the P-38 might stand up with the Zeros in the turns, but we soon found out it couldn't. The differences in tactics in fighting against different types of planes is amazing. In the European theater, the P-38 pilots always made a tight turn as their first maneuver against the Germans. But the maneuver that might save your life against the Germans would mean quick death or at least plenty of trouble against the Japs. A Zero, with its quick maneuverability, can be on the tail of any of our planes in a turn and a half. The P-38 has a very sharp turning angle in relation to its size, but its turns could not begin to match the light Zero's. The P-40 is a lighter ship, but it could never turn with the Zero either.

The latest model of the Zero is quite an airplane. It houses a two thousand horsepower engine. This is equal to the horsepower in our P-47, known as the Thunderbolt, and the Navy ship that was taken over by the Marines, the Vought Corsair. Two thousand horses is a lot of power, as our boys found out the first time they ran into the new Zeros. We had always felt confident that if things got too hot, the P-38's could run away from them. When we put full throttle on, no Zero we had met could stay with us. This feeling of security exploded the first time we ran up against the new Zero.

One day Captain Lowden Enslen, who had been promoted and had taken over the squadron as Commanding Officer when Captain Palmer was removed to Group Headquarters, was leading four planes into Canton and Hong Kong on a dive-bombing mission. They had slammed their bombs into the shipping and were sailing for home when they were jumped by about sixteen Zeros of the new type. Captain Enslen later said the 38's were indicating about 440 miles an hour straight and level, "on the deck" (which means as close to the ground as you can get). They expected to pull right away from the Zeros, but that didn't happen. The new Zero stayed right with our boys for about five minutes, throwing everything they could at them. When the ships finally did break away it was some relief, and about three minutes later Captain Enslen lost his right engine and had to come the rest of the way home on one. He would have been an easy target going along on one engine so close to the ground, but lady luck was with the boys that day.

Lieutenants Billie Beardsley and Machado were on that raid, and the boys spoke long and loudly about the power of the new Zero. In spite of all that power, though, when the four ships were examined not a single bullet could be found in any of them. The Japs must have fired about five thousand rounds of ammunition. Five thousand rounds and not a single hit makes quite a record.

This experience gave us all plenty to think about. We knew we could beat the Japs at altitude in the P-38, but down on the deck we had depended on speed. That factor wouldn't be all in our favor any more. On the other hand, though, I could see in the adventure another proof in support of my contention that the Japs can't shoot.

The missions were continuing to pile up, but the 449th wasn't piling up any terrific score in victories over Jap fighters. We had been selected to do another type of job. That was smacking Jap shipping, the kind of thing that doesn't produce aces, but which hurts the Jap plenty. The low altitude work was dangerous, but so far we had gone ahead without running into too much trouble. Most of our raids had the element of surprise, and as a result we were able to get in and out before the enemy knew we were around. We learned a lot about the Jap in almost every conceivable situation flying these missions, and we now had pretty definite ideas about his fighting ability. We knew he was dangerous, but also we knew he was no superman. Yet the boys were getting a little bit tired. We had been working pretty hard.

The story about the Japs being fanatics to the point of death had been repeated many times and is undoubtedly often true. I had seen a few occasions of it, but more often those 'suicide dives' we heard of were just called that by the Jap propagandists. One incident of this occurred just outside Qualin. A Jap Zero had been shot down by one of the P-40 boys, and the pilot landed in a rice paddy close to the field. The American officers were at the ship almost as soon as it landed to capture the Jap pilot. He was sitting dejectedly beside his ship, waiting to be captured. When the first American officer showed up, the Jap's face lit up and he smiled because the Chinese had not got there before the Americans. He threw his hands up above his head and yelled in clear English, "Don't shoot, me no hara-kiri boy, me no hara-kiri boy!" He was taken to headquarters and questioned. He said he had his fill of the crazy Japs and the war. He was glad to be captured and to be once again with Americans. It seems he had been educated in the States and was in Singapore when the Japs came in. They gave him his choice—fight or get shot. Naturally, he preferred to live, so he fought. He told the intelligence officers all they wanted to know about all the bases he had been on. He said he knew better than to believe all the stuff the Jap soldiers were told about what would happen to him if they were captured. He said the strongest fear dinned into the Jap men is that they will be castrated as soon as they fall into the hands of their enemies. This boy was certainly happy to be among the American forces. The intelligence department got a lot of useful information from him that helped us later on to smash several Jap bases all to smithereens.

General Chennault was a flawless planner when it came to missions, either offensive or defensive. I happened to witness one instance of his defensive planning. The Japs had been sounding off over Radio Tokio that they were coming in to annihilate the American Base Headquarters at Kunming. The General must have just sat back and smiled whenever he heard such threats. The American pilots listened to these Jap radio talks with relish, and practically talked back to the announcer who read the threats. "Come on then, you little yellow-livered bastard, get over here!" For such a raid was a set-up for the American fighters, especially since fighting over your own airdrome is very advantageous in case you do get hit. Well, after they had boasted about so much, the Japs did come in. General Chennault was warned about two hours before they arrived that they were on the way. The P-38's and the P-40's were in the air waiting for them. The Japs had circled the town off in the distance to try and run the fighters out of gas, and they hoped in this way to catch the fighters on the ground

Colonel MacMillan and Lieutenants Williams and Stubbe return from knocking off a few Jap pilots.

refueling. However, General Chennault had thought of that one, too. The fighter planes were fitted with auxiliary fuel tanks which they used up first and then jettisoned. By the time the Japs came in. our fighters were just starting on the gas in their main fuel tanks. One reception committee of P-40's jumped the Zeros some distance away from the field and took them away from the bombers. This left the bombers in the open, and a second squadron of P-40's got on the bombers undisturbed. The Japs said on the radio that they had sent thirty-two bombers on the mission and about fifty Zeros. That night they admitted the loss of thirty-two bombers and ten Zeros. The Americans didn't lose a man. It was quite a day for General Chennault.

On Radio Tokio that night, the announcer said they had lost so-and-so many ships, but that ten Zeros had crashed into military objectives in suicide dives and eight bombers had followed suit. That kind of talk may have gone down with the Japanese people, but as the man from Missouri said, "I was there." I feel quite certain that General Chennault and his staff did not consider the lake outside of town and the mountainside as military objectives, and that they kept their perfect composure as the Japs made their 'suicide dives' into these places. The nearest to the field that a wrecked Jap plane was found was ten miles away. Somehowe, I just seem to doubt the statement that the Japs are all suicide addicts!

It does seem to me, however, that the Jap pilots take plenty of crazy chances. An American pilot would be thought just plain bats if he tried to do the stunts some of them do. American pilots are trained to fly as safely as it is possible to do and still accomplish their objective. That involves a lot of dangerous, daredevil flying, but they aren't supposed to take chances just for the fun of the thing. It is hard to explain why the Japs fly as they do. Maybe the Jap pilots just don't care about life and limb, maybe they are just following their flight leaders. The Zero usually has no armored protection for the pilot, and some of the pilots don't even wear parachutes. We have shot down bombers in the Chinese theater that had Japanese women taking care of the tail gunner's position. The small stature of the women is an advantage in that job because there is so little space for the tail gunner. You hear many stories about the strange actions of the Japs and the weird stunts they pull, usually for no apparent reason. One Jap bomber was shot down, and just before it hit the ground all the occupants jumped out. They must have thought they might have a chance to save their lives that way—but why didn't they have parachutes?

You just start to think that the Jap is a rational being and a pretty good fighter, and then some crazy incident occurs that makes you wonder what kind of people you are fighting, anyway.

But all this is really not the most important point. If the Japs are good fighters on the whole, that's okay with us because it makes it worth our while to prove that we can lick them. If they are a little crazy at times, that's okay with us too, for it hurts them and does us a lot of good. The really important point is something quite different. This is the way I feel about it: After seeing some of the things the Japs have done to our boys, I have a hard time keeping food on my stomach when I read anything in our newspapers about the necessity of having a humane attitude toward the Japs. I am just as humane as the next man. I don't even like to see a dog killed. But when it comes to the Japs, I think they are evil reptiles threatening the foundation of all the good things the American people have spent years of blood, sweat and toil to build. As such, they should be wiped out completely, once and for all. If they escape justice this time, they will come back to cause more misery and grief in the future. The men who know the Japs and their deeds of cunning and torture are fighting hard against them and will clean up on them and win this war. Then it will be time to call the roll of justice.

SQUADRON MORALE AND HUMOR

12

WELL, THE NUMBER OF missions flown kept on growing, and the amount the boys of the 449th learned in flying them was considerable. But all this time, we had to lead some kind of life in between missions, and our activities at our base were many. Naturally, we were somewhat limited. The nearest town was twenty miles away, and it was a typical little Chinese town. There was nothing for us to do there. During all the time I was in China, I went into town three times. The first time, it was for a basketball game with the Chinese, the second I went to see Lee Gregg after he had had his appendix removed, and the third time was to attend midnight mass with the orphans on

Christmas Eve. At that, I guess I went several times more than most of the boys did.

That meant that, although we ranged far and wide on our flying missions, covering hundreds of miles each hour we were in the air, still the social or "normal" part of our lives was remarkably confined. The squadron lived together in one small hostel area that couldn't have covered more than about an acre in all. That and our flying field and its installations were our world. We got plenty of excitement from flying on missions of various kinds, but the only place we could get out and move around was on the ground, after all. Our home for the time being was the base, and we had better like it or we would have to lump it.

It took a lot of harmony between the fellows to make living like this possible at all, and my job as Special Service Officer took on a great deal of importance. To keep some three hundred men occupied during their million spare moments wasn't easy. Our job of flying was demanding and difficult, but it left a good many odd moments to be otherwise occupied. The nervous strain of flying those fast little powerhouses made it doubly necessary to fill in the boys' spare time in agreeable occupations. The Special Service Officer of the 23rd Fighter Group, Major Fred Thompson, was really on the ball. With his help we secured a good library and managed to bring in a film once or twice a week. The schedule of movies was worked out to perfection on paper, but in practice it was always getting disarranged by Jap raids somewhere along the line.

Everybody in camp always went to see the pictures. Even if you had seen the show three or four times already, it always took your mind off your work and put you, in imagination, back home for a while. That way you managed to relax. It didn't matter whether the show was a cowboy thriller or an important dramatic effort, the boys always reacted to it in the same enthusiastic manner, hooting the villain and applauding the hero—not to mention an ear-splitting ovation for the heroine. Even "Harmon of Michigan" would have been a success out there.

Camp shows in China were few and far between. The only man that got to our base in China was Joe E. Brown, whose list of camp tours reads like several of Cook's Grand Tours of the World put together. Joe's show wasn't big, but it was good and funny without getting dirty. The boys like his kind of humor. When he sailed into camp, everybody perked up. His stage was a little hummock—just a slight roll of

Joe E. Brown entertains the boys in China.

the ground—out on the flying field, and for two hours he went through his routine for our boys. How they laughed at his antics! For weeks afterward they remembered everything he did and imitated his stunts. Not the least benefit of having a camp show is that it gives the boys something to write home about. We all thought Joe E. Brown was swell and gave him a rousing vote of thanks.

Our flying schedule was spread out from four a.m. every morning to dusk every evening. While they were out on the flight line waiting for action, or just waiting for something to turn up, the boys got to be a bunch of great bridge enthusiasts. We always played for a murderous limit in order to make the game more interesting. I think that Moonbeam and I were the worst in camp. We often tangled with Stu Rea, who was a shark, and King Mu Wu, our Chinese Intelligence Officer. Wu was a great gambler and a fine boy. His accomplishments in the world of colleges would be enough to bowl anybody over, for he had attended Yale, Harvard and Oxford, and he knew his way around in several different languages. He was a bright kind of fellow. The bridge games would usually get drastic for Moon and me; before long we would find ourselves losing our pants, but we had fun. About half the time while playing bridge was always spent in arguing. That didn't cost Moon and me anything, except that our attention was all the more distracted from the game and so indirectly it may have contributed to our loss.

We also organized various sports while we were up on the line. Most of the boys were more interested in sports than anything else, and volley ball and baseball teams put on many a fast contest. Take an American boy and put him anywhere in the world, and before long you will find a baseball team. That's the way we are built and I guess a typical American boy will always be more interested in knowing who won the World Series than in practically anything else.

At times I would get very worried about the attitude of some of the men. They got homesick, and you could read their faces like a book. Letters wouldn't arrive on time, or maybe some mail would get lost, and their dejection knew no bounds. Then word would come through from their folks or their sweetheart and things would brighten up again. If the folks at home could see the difference their letters make for their boys overseas, they would see to it that the boys get a letter every single day.

When it comes to this question of morale it is amazing to see how the boys react to every little incident that breaks the monotony of their routine. They are particularly grateful for anything funny happening in their midst. In this our camp was just like any other. We always managed to find something to laugh about. And sometimes the things that happened were really amazing and then some.

One time, for instance, Lieutenants Lee Gregg and Zeke Weber were out on a mission over Canton, acting as top cover for four of our planes that were dive-bombing the docks. This was Zeke's first mission, so it was a big day for him. He was flying as Gregg's wingman. Gregg and Weber both spotted two Zeros over our dive-bombers, so they started down on them. As they approached they saw there were not two, but sixteen Zeros on the scene. There are times when it is best to run instead of fight, and this was one of those times. The dive-bombers got off the target and went for home. Gregg and Weber circled a few times and then happened to spot one lone Zero. Most of the sixteen had taken off in pursuit of the dive-bombing planes. Gregg made a pass at the Zero and put a few bursts into him, but the Zero turned and got on their tail. Gregg called Weber on the interphone and said, "Zeke, you turn right and I'll turn left and we'll trap this little bastard." It was a good signal, but Weber had lost his radio. Gregg turned, Weber turned with him, and the Zero aimed at Gregg and hit Weber. After a few minutes Gregg got a pass at the Zero and knocked him down, but not before poor Weber's plane looked like a sieve. Weber made one of our bases and refueled in order to get back to home base. When he finally landed on our field, and his wheels hit the ground, it was like the wonderful one-hoss shay. All the cables on his plane snapped at once. If he had been in the air all would have been over, but as it was, he rolled down the runway with his rudder and ailerons flapping in the wind while the boys on the field watched with amazement. It was quite a sight. You would have sworn that thing flapping down the runway was a cackling hen and not the U.S. Army's proudest fighter plane. After we had gotten over the excitement we began to see the funny side of it, and Gregg and Weber have been kidded plenty about that day's work.

Another necessity of life for the boys in the army is that they must have a chance to grumble. Any good Army man can complain. He has the know-how it takes for a real, thorough-going, straight from the shoulder gripe. It's one of the skills a man learns in the army. Of course, the complaints must not be about a very serious matter. That is not part of the game. The rule is, the bigger, better, more really rousing a gripe, the smaller its object must be. Now our boys were really getting good at this old army technique. First of all, it was agreed that ours was the best damn outfit in the world. That was that. But hell's bells, there was absolutely nothing that wasn't wrong with us and our base.

Two of the boys were sort of on the spot in a professional way. Dave Williams was our Post Exchange Officer, and everyone tried to wheedle cigarettes out of him, or a candy bar if possible. Dave was one of our loyal Texans, and every time the Texas argument came up, Dave was soon joined by Tommy Taylor and Bill Beardsley. As Post Exchange Officer he took plenty, and as a Texan he took some more. Earl Helms was our Mess Officer, and he did a swell job of it. He had stacks of kidding complaints all the time, and took an awful beating on the subject of how we liked our food, but he was the kind of fellow who didn't let it get under his skin and sent back as good as he got. He could always threaten to give us Spam, so he really had the whip hand all the time. One of the funniest scenes around camp was the spectacle of Earl in an argument with the Chinese cooks. It was even funnier when you considered that neither party to the argument understood what the other was talking about.

The missions had been changed a bit. We were actually given the chance to plan them ourselves! It was one of the breaks that started us on our way to pile up a real score. Bill Bolton and Earl Helms planned a mission just for the two of them. They decided to go North and look for trains to strafe. Each one carried a five hundred pound bomb under his wing for good measure. Together they caused enough trouble for a dozen men. Bolton made a direct hit on a large boat and also damaged the docks it was in with his one bomb, and Helms got three iron smelters. After this they went up the railroads and got three trains apiece. Then they found a Radar station and proceeded to put that out of commission. They returned to base safe and sound without seeing an enemy plane. One of the curious things that happened on this mission was that Helms had put several holes in Bolton's ship. Bolton would peel off to go after the train and Helms would follow. Then Helms would fire at the engine, the bullets would ricochet and go through Bolton's ship. They had quite a trip, though, in spite of Bolton's bullet holes. For this day's work, Bill Bolton was awarded the Silver Star..

During this same day's work, a good crack was heard over the interphones of the planes. A group of P-40's had gone up north with Helms and Bolton. When they got to the railway, the P-38's went north and the P-40's south along the line. The 40's found no trains, but a lot of Zeros. The fight was in rapid progress, and one of the boys had apparently lost his wingman. This conversation came in over the phones. "Hey, Bill, where are you?" A moment later the reply was heard, "Here I am, down here in the pass. Come on down, I've got six of these little bastards trapped!" I guess his buddy went down and rescued him from those six Zeros he had trapped, but everybody got a laugh out of his crack. Trapping a Zero is such an impossible job anyway that mentioning it calmly in a situation like that just about threw the boys.

When the weather in China gets bad it doesn't fool. It really means it, and is likely to mean it for days on end. When the weather is bad in China, even the birds don't fly. During spells like these, the squadron would always throw a party. The drink served on these occasions was supplied by the men, and was a Chinese wine the boys had named "jing-bao" juice. The words "jing bao" mean "Jap air raid," so you can draw your own conclusion about what the stuff tasted like. I often saw the results of the juice, and it always appeared to me to be more disastrous than any Jap air raid going. The drink comes in various colors and various prices. The white kind is called "white lightning" by the boys and is rather special, for the more usual color is red. It has sort of a sweetish, winey taste. These parties always developed into speech contests between Schultz and Moon. It was a close race to see who could make the most speeches in one night. The evening would invariably end up with everyone trying to throw everyone else into a rice paddy. There were times when it was quite unnecessary to worry about throwing anyone in, for most of the boys would just walk in by themselves. This was why we nicknamed Schultz the "Rice Paddy Boy." He got lost for one whole night, and then next morning we found him sleeping peacefully out in the paddy. The juice had been strong that night.

The boys were doing a different type of work in China from what they had done in Africa. Back there, the P-38's were mostly used for top cover and protection for the bombers. In China, interception was our line. In Africa, a man wasn't known for the number of victories he had chalked up, but for his all-round flying ability. I knew quite a few boys in Africa who had flown fifty missions over enemy territory and never had a victory. That wasn't what they were out for. But they were men who could always be counted on to get there and to get back. They may not have shot down any enemy planes, but neither did they have any holes in their own. They just did their job and came home. In China, the situation was different. Victories counted. And a squadron's success was measured that way.

We had some swell fighters in the 449th, and we had our share of victories, even though so many of our missions had been of the variety where we didn't tangle with enemy fighters. Two of the best were Kendall Dowis and Gerry Hammond. After seeing Dowis fly in combat, I would be willing to swear the man must have ice-water in his veins. He was always master of the situation, whatever it might be, and there were a lot of possibilities. Gerry Hammond came from Ypsilanti, Michigan, and was practically a neighbor of mine, although we had to go to China to meet each other. We had both been in the same class in college, and we went into the Army at the same time. The boys had tagged the name of "Moe" on Gerry, because he was a champion griper, always complaining about everything but never serious. He had more fun griping about things than any other two guys, but in the air he was all business.

Earl Helms and the boys were sitting in our room one evening talking to the new flight nurse. The boys had not seen an American girl for ages, and naturally Maggie Miller was a great help to squadron morale. The chance to talk to a girl who is from home, who can say hello to you in a good, cheery way, and who understands English, seems like a miracle to you after you've been away from home as long as we had. Maggie had only been with us for about a week. We hadn't got used to the fact that we had a girl in our midst and the slight revision of our customs that seemed to be called for on account of her presence was not as yet firmly entrenched. That night the room was busy, everyone was talking, the phonograph was going, when in walked a vision from the shower room. It was one of the boys who had obviously forgotten that Maggie was around. He had just taken a shower and was wearing a derby hat and a pair of heavy winter flying boots. Nothing else. Maggie looked up casually, then gulped and looked away. The room suddenly became very quiet, but the boy with the derby still didn't realize she was there. Then Helms yelled at him, "Well?" and suddenly our derby-man bolted for the door. It was about two weeks before he gave up running in the opposite direction whenever the squadron nurse came along. Hammond and Dowis in particular never got over that one, and they didn't let the poor clown who pulled it forget about it, either.

Every now and then our Chinese friends would throw a party for us, and some of the fondest memories we have are of these affairs. The Chinese believe in simple living, but when they have guests they go all out to entertain them. They drink their drinks out of a small cup that resembles a demitasse. They stand up and point their cups at you and say "Gombay!" This means bottoms up. If you have ever attended such a gathering, you know that to attempt to drink with the Chinese drink for drink is sudden death. They always honor the officers acording to rank. As second lieutenants we didn't draw much water, and this was okay with us. The squadron commander would invariably be put away early in the evening. They would accomplish this in a quick way. There were large circular tables, at which about ten Chinese officers and one American were seated. Each Chinese officer would drink a toast to the American guest, and in China when a toast is made it is an individual affair between the man who is making the toast and the toastee. In China, if someone toasts you, you have to stand up and the two of you drink the drink. Before long the American officer had been toasted ten times by the Chinese officers, which meant ten drinks to one for each of the Chinese, and the lights soon went out in the American section. The boys always remembered going to these parties—but few ever remembered coming home.

The Chinese boys were good, all-round pals, and we had a lot of fun with them in a lot of ways. One of our favorite sports was basketball, and we would often take on the Chinese team for a fast game. The Chinese excel at this game. Perhaps on a large court playing under the standard regulations they might be beaten by a rangy American team, but on those mud outdoor courts they really gave us a lesson. They were small, fast and in top condition, and were some opponents. Chinese rules for basketball differ a little from ours, but basically it's the same game. They use a larger ball but have a smaller hoop on the basket, for one thing. The good-will of the American team was often put to the test in these games, for the boys couldn't help getting sore now and then when the Chinese had them wrapped into knots. Fists would start flying and international friendship would seem to be at stake for a minute or two. There was never a real fight, it only meant that the game sometimes got a bit rough. The Chinese were fine athletes and good competitors and sportsmen. Crowds of their friends always turned out to see the sport and cheered for them as though it was a Rose Bowl game.

The nicknames that got tagged onto various boys in the squadron all had their stories. Living together as we did, almost as though we were on an island of our own there in the middle of the great Chinese landscape, it was inevitable that we got to know each other pretty well, and especially we got to know everybody's funny points, his sore spots, his weaknesses. And all these things got ribbed plenty, and were the sources of many nicknames.

Lieutenant Alfred Yorsteon Jr. was always known as "Pappy" to the boys. He had got married before coming overseas, and was anxiously expecting the news of a new arrival in his family. He had bet just about everybody in the squadron that it would be a boy. One fine day the long awaited cable came. Pappy's excitement and bets had infected some of the other boys, and they could not refrain from peeking at the cable. The cable said the new baby was a boy. Now all these jokers had bet it would be a girl, so they calmly changed the cable to that effect. Pappy was happy anyway to hear it was a baby, and cheerfully paid off his bets of soft drinks and cigarettes, and everybody had a marvelous time. The matter was cleared up a day or two later, and Pappy collected his drinks and cigarettes back again with interest.

Johnny Opsvig was known as "The General," or just plain General Opsvig, because he always told everyone what to do. We granted him that privilege, though, after the day over Canton when he bagged his first Zero with a 90 degree deflection shot, the shot most difficult to make in aerial gunnery.

My own nickname was T-Bone, but I shall not explain why. The squadron Shakespeare was Chuck Longueil, who was interested in things like literature and classical music. He would often get into long dissertations about classical music in the room with Helms and Bolton and me. Helms and I would put in a heart-felt plea to him and Bolton to get off the higher plane and come down to earth with some good ole swing music. Chuck Longueil didn't say much aside from these long-haired discussions, but his flying proved that he took a back seat to few when it came to really important matters.

Lieutenant Keith Newnom was nicknamed Boots. I don't think Boots could have weighed ninety-five pounds dripping wet, but he was always trying to throw Bill Beardsley into a rice paddy at the parties. "The Lord" Beardsley, as Bill had been dubbed, was a little fellow of about twice Boots' size, and must have weighed practically two hundred. One of the scenes I remember most vividly is that of Beardsley holding onto a table leg, with little Boots trying vainly to pry him loose. They looked like a terrier and a bear in a friendly tussle.

Some of the incidents that seemed funny to us after they were over

(*Above*) The pilots wait for a Jap alert. (*Below*)
"Ripper" Rea holds up a jeep in front of the mess hall.

were really pretty close shaves. There is a special sort of hilarity about absurd and narrow escapes that I think fliers develop. A lot of our humor dealt with stuff that would have been tragedy if it had been just a hair's breadth different, but as it was it somehow seemed quite a joke to us.

One day Lee Gregg dove down on a ship at Canton and had strafed the whole deck before he saw that it was a destroyer. Now, strafing a destroyer is like putting your neck into a noose, because they carry more flak guns than anything else on earth. Nobody in his right mind would go down and strafe one of those babies, not if he was watching what he was doing. That was funny in sort of the same way it is funny when Charlie Chaplin strolls nonchalantly down a path toward a canyon reading a newspaper, and calmly walks over a narrow plank bridge across the chasm, still deeply absorbed in his paper. On the other side he looks up, sees the bridge he has just walked across, and falls down in a panic.

The week after this exploit, Gregg had an attack of appendicitis and the Doc said he would have to take out his appendix. The Doc's assistant was a little private by the name of Donnegan who had been a private nurse before the war. He worked like a horse and was always looking after the boys. Gregg was lying on his bed in our room when Donnegan came in to see him. Donnegan happened to be carrying a scalpel which he had meant to leave in the sterilizer in the Doc's office and I must admit it looked pretty wicked there in his hand. Donnegan just wanted to have a look at Gregg's side. The light was bad in the room, and Gerry Hammond and Helms and I were all in bed too. Donnegan started for Hammond's bed by mistake, and Hammond seeing that knife, leaped out of bed, mosquito netting and all, and started climbing out of the window. We turned the light on. Gregg just lay back on his bed and pulled up his shirt. He thought Donnegan was going to take out his appendix then and there, and he was ready for it. "Well, come on, take it out, don't stall around," he said calmly. After that, we were positive that not even a battleship would faze Gregg.

One day while we were on the alert for Jap planes we had some B-25's come in to the field to gas up for a mission. The Commander of this flight of B-25's was a full Colonel. They landed just before noon and went up to the hostel area for lunch. We had a cook who was known far and wide among the army boys for his ability to make good pie, which attracted many customers. On this particular day, Earl Helms was up on a test flight with his ship. After lunch the Colonel was just driving down to the field to take off again when Helms made a turn into the field. Suddenly Helms accidentally tripped his machine guns. The Colonel stopped the car and dove into a rice paddy filled with water, under the impression it was a Jap strafing raid. The Colonel had a good outfit on, too. It was kind of hard on the Colonel, and Helms wasn't allowed by the boys to forget that one. I don't know if Helms ever felt like telling a superior officer to go jump in the lake, but just that one time, at least, he actually made one do it.

Helms was one of the lucky boys who had got all his clothes through to China, as his stuff hadn't been on the downed transport. As a consequence, his stock of clothing became more or less the common property of his less fortunate buddies. It was tough on all of us that Earl only had one bathrobe, because our room contained six men who all needed to wear it at approximately the same time. With nurses present in the vicinity, we couldn't go traipsing around in the raw very well. Luckily for me, Earl and I were about the same size, and the bathrobe fitted me well. On little Gerry Hammond it looked like a tent, but he didn't mind. He took his turn wearing it, every morning, like everybody else.

And so things went on . . .

We didn't have many luxuries, but we had enough of what it takes to keep up the old morale, and we had a sense of humor that was sometimes screwy but always functioned. The men in the 449th were one swell gang, and before they are done they will make both Hitler and Hirohito sorry they ever even opened their yaps.

KIUKIANG ! ! !

13

THE ACTIVITIES OF THE squadron had slowed down quite a bit during the month of October, 1943, because of the weather. The early part of the month had been fine, and we had been able to make some good raids on the Japs. Then the weather ganged up on us, and only a small percentage of the boys had been able to get in their flying time for the month.

We never took to the air just to practice or to get in flying time.

When we flew, it was on serious business, which meant combat or, occasionally, an official mission for other purposes. General Chennault had emphasized the shortage of gasoline when we first talked with him, and we took that shortage seriously. We had enough for the really necessary work of the squadron, but none whatever to play around with. Every drop of gasoline we used was brought in under difficult conditions, and it had to be made to count. The Japs put in a lot of effort just to get us to use up gas, sometimes sending out missions with no other purpose than to get our planes into the air. We ran into this stratagem of theirs more than once. We would wait until they were close enough to warrant our taking off, and then we would go up to meet them, only to have them make a 180 degree turn and go home to their bases. They never caught us out of gas, though, and General Chennault's use of extra tanks on the P-38's and P-40's made us able to stay up there when necessary in order to get them when they finally came in. The Japs never caught our planes on the ground except on a couple of occasions, and then it was because of a failure of the warning system, not because we had been forced to come down to refuel.

So we had a lull in flying during most of the month of October. We had plenty of time for card games and reading, but that didn't make up to us for not flying. The weather kept on getting worse instead of better, it seemed to us in our impatience. Although it was the monsoon season, our weather officer said that this spell of fog and low ceilings was not due to that, but was simply caused by a cold front. At first we hadn't minded it so much, because the squadron had been flying a pretty heavy schedule and the boys were tired, but as the days went on we got rested and ready to go.

It was during this spell of rotten weather that a couple of top-notch correspondents visited our base. Eric Severeid, of Columbia Broadcasting, was one of them. He had been on the plane that crashed with all our clothes just over the Hump. When I was introduced to Severeid, he said, "Harmon, yes, I seem to remember the name. I think it was on a bag I threw out of the plane that day." He was a swell fellow, and so was Brooks Atkinson of the *New York Times,* who was with him. The two correspondents were with us about three days, and it was a pleasure to have them around. They had traveled recently and could give us a good description of the situation on the other fronts. We were hungry for first-hand news, and the bull sessions were long and loud during their stay with the 449th.

The longest discussion was the one about the comparative dangers of different kinds of missions. According to the boys, strafing and skip-bombing topped the list. The consensus of opinion was that we had nothing much to worry about with Jap fighters so long as the fight was anywhere near even. That was a condition we hardly ever saw in China where the Japs always outnumbered us. But even so, it was generally agreed that low level work was considerably more dangerous than getting involved in any sort of dog-fight. That settled, we went on and covered the state of the world and the progress of the war, and I guess we solved more problems that night than Congress can manage to take cognizance of in two or three of its stormiest sessions.

The events of that night and the following few days stand out in my memory with unusual clarity. There were so many little things that didn't seem particularly important at the time when they happened, but somehow I can't help associating them with later events and in looking back it seems to me that we might have understood them as warning signals of Fate. One of these little things is the fact that we were so very outspoken that night in our contempt of Jap fighters and the danger they constituted for us.

On the afternoon of October 29th old man Sun finally broke through the overcast. It was sure a swell sight to see him shining brightly up there again. It meant a lot to us, for if you ever want to see a fidgety bundle of nerves, just take a look at a flier who is grounded. Now we would fly again and Captain Enslen was quick to take advantage of the improved weather conditions.

The Japs up north around Hankow, Wuchang and Kiukiang had been given quite a bit of rest because of the bad weather. It was high time we let them know we were still alive. Luckily for me, I was on the alert that day, and I welcomed the chance to take the mission which meant that I could bolster my flying time for that month a bit. The rest of the boys of course felt the same way about it. After checking his date, Captain Enslen decided that if we didn't have a mission from head-quarters, we would look for shipping in the Yangtze near Kiukiang. We had received reports from Intelligence that there were some pretty big boats on the river in that area, and if we could damage the Jap supply line it would be a good mission and a feather in our war-bonnet. The boys had been in the area several times and had run into very little flak and hardly any fighters at all.

We were briefed by Captain Enslen and Lieutenant Wu, our Intelligence officer, and the mission was planned. We would take nine ships, five dive bombers each carrying a five hundred pound bomb under its wing, and four planes as top cover. Schultz was given the lead plane in the cover with Lieutenant Robbins flying his wing. Lieutenant Tommy Taylor was my element leader and I was flying in the last position, or what is known as "tail-end Charlie." Captain Enslen was the lead dive bomber, with Lieutenant Robinson on his wing. Ripper Rea was the second element leader and Lieutenant Weber was on his wing. Kendall Dowis, old reliable himself, was the fifth of the dive bombers. Dowis and Rea had earned quite a reputation for being able to lay their bombs right on the target, and when it came to coolness under fire, they were like ice. The nine of us went to the mess hall to get something to eat while the crew chiefs and the ground men loaded the bombs and readied the planes for action. When we came back to the field fortified with the chef's best, the planes were ready to go and so were we.

Then Captain Enslen consulted the time charts again and decided it was too late to make it that afternoon, after all. It had taken us too long to have everything in readiness, and we couldn't make our target and get back to base before nightfall. China was difficult enough to navigate in broad daylight, and at night it was next to impossible for our fighter planes. So the mission was called off. The bombs had to be taken off the wings of our planes again, for the ships would have to be ready if we had an early morning alert.

However, the boys wanted to fly that mission pretty badly, now it had all been planned, and so it was decided that unless we had an alert or heard from headquarters assigning us another mission, we would carry out our plans for Kiukiang the next morning. It would have been wiser to think up something entirely new.

The following morning we were on the field at dawn as usual. We watched the plotting board faithfully, and there were no reports of the Japs coming in anywhere. We waited until eight o'clock. When we had not heard from headquarters by that time, we knew that the big bombers were not going out that day and that we would not be needed for escort or other duties. So we were all clear to go on the mission we had planned.

Once again Captain Enslen briefed us on our targets. The bombs were loaded while we had breakfast in the mess hall. I drove back to the line with Doc Burns in his jeep. On the way I remarked to the Doc what a swell pair of gloves he was wearing that day. It was a nippy morning, and he insisted I should wear his gloves on the mission and return them when I came back. I hadn't been hinting, but something about it all made me accept the offer. I couldn't say why.

As we gathered in the ready room, I found that Lieutenant Helms had borrowed my parachute. I searched around for another and finally grabbed old Moonbeam's. Moon was the only other guy who was big enough to have a chute that would do for me. When I started out for my plane, Moon and the Doc yelled something about bailing out. I turned around and replied, "Let's not talk like that, boys, once is enough for the T-bone." I went on out to my ship and crawled in. My crew chief was on the wing and gave me a pat on the back. He said, "Give 'em hell, Lieutenant, and get one of those little bastards for me." I guess he must have said something like that often before we went off, but I remember it only for this particular time. I remember exactly how he said it, word for word.

I waved the crew chief off my wing and started the engines. We taxied to the end of the runway, then Captain Enslen started down the runway on his take-off. I was to be the last man off, so I sat and watched the boys sail into the clear blue sky of the morning of October 30th. It sure seemed strange to me. I just happened to think, today was the first anniversaary of my wings. Who would have thought so much could have happened in the short space of a year? It was an important day for me. Lieutenant Taylor waggled his ailerons and I waggled back. We started down the runway together.

No sooner had we gotten into the air than we heard the frantic voice of Moon on the interphone. Lieutenant Robinson, who was flying Captain Enslen's wing, had blown his nose-wheel tire on the take-off. Moon, ever watchful, had seen the tire go. Luckily Robinson had made it okay into the air, but it had been a ticklish situation for a moment considering that he had a five hundred pound bomb under his right wing. If that baby had gone off, there would have been very little left of Robinson and the seven P-38's following him, for we were all pretty close together on the formation take-off. Moon instructed Robinson to go out in the mountains and drop his bomb safely, then return and make a belly landing. Robinson did as he was ordered and returned to the field. He made a perfect belly landing, and the ship was ready to fly again in a short time. His having to leave the formation reduced the flight to eight ships. Eight Lightnings were out to give Hirohito a belt in one of his sore spots, his crowded supply ships.

Rather than take any chances, Captain Enslen decided to go to one of our front line bases farther north to gas up before leaving on the final lap of our mission. This would be a long flight and a good one. If we ran into much of a fight, we would need the extra gas to get home on, that was sure. As we circled in and landed at the other base, Lieutenant Taylor almost dipped his wing into the ground because the haze at the field was so bad and his ship was caught in the propwash, these violent wind currents caused by the plane landing just ahead of him. He made it in okay, because he is one damn good flier and knows his way around a tight spot, but it was a bad moment and another narrow escape.

While our planes were gassed up Taylor and I got together and made a few last minute plans. They had to do with the Intelligence report we got at this forward base that two Jap planes were patrolling the area. The thought of catching those two Zeros made the boys who were flying protection raring to get into the air. Maybe today would be the day we would catch the Japs with their pants down, maybe today the odds would be on our side. Maybe they would!

After taking off again Captain Enslen set the course. Our trim planes went sailing over those mountains like birds. After about an hour, I noticed that I had been siphoning gas out of my left tank. I called Taylor and asked him to circle around and check up on it. He did and said he could see nothing. I was sure then that the trouble must be in my gas system, and after changing it a few times it caught and the siphoning stopped. I didn't much like the idea of playing tag with the Zeros without all the gas I could get, so I was glad it seemed to be adjusted. We flew on, and as usual when the high point of a mission is at hand, everyone was tense and tight. Every time a mike button clicked you could have sworn the canopy of each plane jumped a foot. Everyone was alert and ready for the Japs. As planned, we headed for the Yangtze just below Hankow. It was our idea to come up to the river and pick off any boats we saw down below. If no boats were on the river, our objectives would be the rice "go-downs," which are the big grain storehouses, and the gasoline dump at the Jap airfield at Kiukiang. As we approached the target the morning looked calm and peaceful. Schultz and Robbins began to weave over the dive bombers, and Taylor and I followed suit. The dive bombers had gone in at about six thousand feet, and we were at about eight thousand feet protecting them. As Kiukiang came into sight, we saw that all the streets were cleared and that there was no sign at all of activity on the ground. The Japs had been warned!

Sitting out at the docks just off the harbor of the town was a large transport steamer. This was our meat, we had caught a swell target for dive bombers. The bombers started their runs.

The mike clicked and Schultz's voice said, "Six Zeros at three o'clock!" So there were six, not two.

We were in a slight turn to the left at the moment, and sure enough there were six of the ugly little devils off the right wing about a thousand feet above us. The dive bombers had started their run and our job was to protect them. As Schultz called out his warning, I reached to release my belly tanks and cocked up on my left wing to look behind me. Coming down at us from above were six more Zeros. That made twelve altogether. I punched the mike button and called out, "Six more Zeros at nine o'clock," I looked at Schultz and Robbins and Taylor, and saw they were headed up into the first six Zeros that Schultz had called out. I was trying to release my belly tank, but I don't think it came off, for I didn't feel the ship kick.

At the same time I turned into the six Zeros behind me and fired a short burst. The Japs didn't like the idea of taking on a P-38 at head-on range, so they busted up. They were flying in groups of threes instead of twos, as we did. The leading three turned left and dove. The three on the right scattered. The first two of them turned right and dove, while the third one turned left and dove alone. I was practically lined up with him and we were both diving. I cut loose with the machine guns and the first burst was a lucky shot. It tore the canopy right off the little fellow over there and his motor burst into flames. When I saw this I pressed the cannon button, and the Zero went straight down.

The air now sounded like a million buzzing bees, as the motors wound up and the ships started around each other. Added to the infernal noise came at irregular intervals the sharp brrrrrrrr-upp, brup, brrr-upp of the machine guns of all the ships. I didn't see our dive bombers come off the target, so I climbed back looking for another Zero. Over the lake down below there was another one climbing upward. My dive had made my airspeed very high, and I closed in on the climbing Zero. I don't think he saw me, because I came right up under his wing and fired a short burst. The shot caught him close to the fuselage and a part of his wing tore off. We closed right in and everything cut loose. The Zero blew up.

I had climbed steeply in this encounter and was just going to pull over and head for home. Then I heard a sharp ring against the armor plating behind me. Almost immediately a second shot hit the armor plate under my seat and I was given a slight jolt. The third shot exploded between my legs. This one blew the gas primer out and blew my legs off the rudder pedals. Later on I discovered my pant legs were blown off at the knee. How I ever missed catching some of those shell splinters I'll never know. The gas primer was now blown clean out and the gas line in the cockpit was on fire. I reached down between my legs and tried to stamp out the fire with my hands. "This is hard on Doc Burns' gloves," I thought and tried again. It was a useless gesture. The fire only grew in intensity. The flames began to lick my face and arms and legs.

My plane was now in a ninety degree dive straight for the lake. I knew that I had gone into that dive at about eight thousand feet, but I didn't know how much altitude I had lost while I was trying to put out the flames. I did know for sure that to stay in that cockpit very much longer would mean roasting alive, so I loosened my safety belt and jettisoned the canopy.

The terrific rate of speed the ship had built up in its dive had caused a great suction in the cockpit, and I was literally torn out of the ship. Not being sure of my altitude, I pulled the ripcord on my chute almost at once. As soon as I had done that I was sorry, for I had heard about how the Japs had machine-gunned parachuting pilots, and I knew the correct move was to pull a delayed fall and open your chute as late as possible. The trouble was, I didn't know what was "as late as possible." My chute opened with a jerk, and I snapped upright under it.

The first sight that met my eyes after I had come to was a P-38 going by, hell-bent for election towards home with two Zeros on his tail throwing enough lead at him to sink a battleship. It was Schultz. I was sure I recognized that Golden Eagle. As I found out later, he had tried to shoot his way through the first formation and almost made it. His first shot had picked off the Zero flight leader, that fellow had tried to dodge the Eagle's burst but in the attempt he had pulled into his wingman. They both went down and Schultz had two victories with one burst. After that Schultz had been in it hot and heavy. Lieutenant Robbins had picked off a Zero that had been on Schultz's tail but in doing so had been shot down himself. After that Schultz made off for home praying like a man with the devil on his tail.

After Schultz had zoomed by, I looked off to my left and saw a Zero circling me. Directly opposite him, another Zero also began to circle around my chute. At that moment my heart went right up into throat. A man in a parachute is as helpless against a strafing plane as a duck on a string.

I had heard machine gun bursts, and I decided the only hope for me was to play dead. I folded over in my harness and hung limp. Out of the side of my eyes I could see the two Zeros still slowing down to continue their circle. I was waiting for them to turn into me any minute and start blazing away. During those moments I was undoubtedly setting the world's record for "Hail Mary's." I must have said a million. The moments seemed to drag by. There wasn't a breath of air stirring in the sky that day, and it seemed as if the chute would never reach the ground.

Looking below I could see that if I didn't pull my shroud lines I would be in for a ducking in the lake. I thought about it, and decided that I would rather take a ducking any day than a fifty caliber bullet through the stomach. The Zeros kept circling slowly, and the suspense was worse than any I have ever experienced.

At last the lake came up to meet me. The Japs hadn't shot! Why they didn't I couldn't imagine.

Since I had been unable to unstrap my leg straps, I knew I was taking a chance of having the chute fall on me while I was in the water and perhaps drown me. However, this didn't worry me too much at this point. I took a deep breath and went under water. While under the surface, I unbuckled my straps with one hand and held onto the rubber inflated cushion that was on my chute. This acted as a buoy and was strong enough to hold me up. I came up under the chute, which was now on the surface of the lake, and grabbed a breath of air. My lungs had seemed almost about to burst, but I knew I was still out of sight of the two Zeros. They made three dives on the chute, and each time I heard them starting down, I would go under the water and under the chute. They must have thought I was dead, because they went back to their base after that. What a relief when I poked my head out from under the edge of that chute and saw them winging away into the distance!

Well, I had come through that one all right! I was still alive and with some luck I might be eating fish heads and rice until the end of the war. If I used my head in addition to having luck I might do even better, but I knew that was asking a lot, being as far behind the enemy's line as I knew I must be.

Now, for the first time, I realized that I was burned, and pretty badly. It hurt, but I wasn't going to let that bother me if I could help it. With the relief at escaping from those Zeros that had come down after me the old thinking machine started to function again, and I began making some plans. I was still there in the water hanging on to my rubber cushion and thinking like hell. I had heard enough about the Jap ways of torturing their prisoners, and I didn't relish the idea of being kicked around by those yellow-livered little supermen. I would be damned if I would go out of the picture without taking a few of the Japs with me. I still had my forty-five, and I definitely decided on a fight, regardless of what happened. The chance of getting treated decently if you were captured was a laugh. That possibility, I thought, I might as well write off here and now, and so I began figuring things out for drastic action.

It was thirty-two days before I got back to my base again. In those thirty-two days, I went through the most physically painful experience of my life. The burns on my legs and face got infected and festering. Medical aid in China outside army bases is unheard of and so there was only one remedy available for me. That was cold tea. The tannic acid is supposed to take the sting out of the burns and help them to heal. It did help some, but the results were far from perfect. My face was so badly burned that eyes and lips were simply swollen shut. I had just barely been able to peer out from between my lids when I came down, but soon they were completely cracked and closed. Because my mouth was also burned badly, I could hardly eat for seventeen days.

That trip taught me an awful lot. One of my main supports was prayer, and never for one moment did I lose the faith that Mom had always taught me to have. And Faith proved a stronger weapon than a Tommy gun or any other man-made arm. While I was on the trip back I once again picked up that ole curse of amoebic dysentery. That in itself would be enough to make a man miserable, but at the same time I had those nice little burns to bother me and really, I just didn't care anymore if hell itself froze over.

I lost fifty-two pounds in those thirty-two days. My weight is usually round about two hundred pounds, but I weighed in at a strapping one hundred and forty-seven when I got back. Scarecrow would have been the word. I hadn't weighed that little since I was a kid in high school.

That day early in December of the year 1943 when I climbed out of a plane back at my home base is something I'll never forget. The world had never looked rosier. I was home. Back with the boys that I knew like brothers. I was met by Moon, Doc Burns and the camp chaplain, Father Joe Cosgrove. I was so happy, I started to cry.

The base had changed a good deal. I hardly recognized the place. We had new pilots and a new commanding officer. Captain Enslen was dead. Taylor and Robbins were listed as "missing in action." Just as I had been listed as "missing in action" for thirty-two days. Captain Enslen, I learned, had been rescued badly wounded after the fight, but he had died of pneumonia about ten days later. In him the 449th had lost a great squadron leader and a fine flier. Robbins and Taylor were reported to be on their way out. These losses came as a shock to me, for I had only seen one ship smoking in the fight, that had been Lieutenant Robbins'. I hadn't seen Taylor or Captain Enslen in the fight at all after the first break.

The squadron was very cut up about these losses, but none of the boys had ever lost confidence that their buddies would come walking out of the Chinese plain one fine day. They had gone on about their business and had really made up for the disastrous day at Kiukiang in a smashing raid on Formosa. I was still walking out of enemy territory when that raid was pulled, so I couldn't be in on it, but it gave me a lift when I heard about the success. They had accounted for some twenty planes in the air and several more on the ground, and hadn't lost a single man in the action. Schultz had added two and Moon three to their string that day.

When I walked up to the barracks the afternoon of my return I felt a warm glow inside my chest. I felt that every man at the base was glad to see me back! The warm smiles and heartfelt handshakes that greeted me were nothing to the expression in the boys' eyes. My crew chief and the ground men really gave me a welcome, and it was the first time I really understood what those boys mean to a pilot and what the pilot means to them. They set up the punch that the pilot delivers, and it makes a close bond. I looked quite a sight in my Chinese clothes, and all the boys were snapping pictures of me.

Then I saw old Schultz coming down the steps. He had spotted me and broke into a dead run. Boy, what a reunion! We both started to cry. I was happy as hell that he had got out. The last time I had seen him, his position hadn't looked too good.

Late that afternoon, Father Cosgrove said a thanksgiving mass in honor of my return. I think that I am a pretty hard guy, but I felt like bawling like a baby. When I looked around at the men crowded into that recreation room, Catholic and non-Catholic alike, taking part in this mass of thanksgiving, I could just have thrown in the towel. Nothing, absolutely nothing in my life, has ever equaled that moment.

Father Cosgrove said mass the following night for Captain Enslen, and the whole squadron again attended. There may have been men

Harmon reunited with Major Burns, Bob Schultz, and Ryan Moon after being lost for thirty-two days.

This quilted suit that Harmon wore when he returned to his China base is the uniform of the Chinese soldier.

there who had never been inside a church in their lives, but that night they were all there paying their individual respects to the memory of our dead Commanding Officer, and asking in their own words that the Big Boss upstairs might hear their prayers for Ens and the rest of the boys who had flown their last flight for the 449th.

On the day of my return, after the thanksgiving mass, we went over to the dining hall for the banquet. "Monaghan's mealy mess," as it was now called in honor of the new mess officer, Tom Monaghan, really outdid itself that night. The boys had been tipped off that I was coming, and the banquet that was lined up to celebrate the occasion was a real feast. I was also much impressed by the dressiness of the affair. All the officers were dressed in pinks or greens and at first I couldn't imagine where they had dug them up. I knew that twenty of them had lost all their uniforms in the same crash that had accounted for mine. After considerable kidding around, they finally admitted they had borrowed their handsome outfits from the new replacement pilots. Tom Monaghan really had his Chinese cooks on the ball that night. It was a meal fit for a king; I took the lion's share, which means that I ate like a horse. It was the first time in quite a while that food had really tasted good to me. The "jing-bao" juice flowed freely, and once again Schultz and Moon were trying to see who could make the most speeches. The language was somewhat more refined, now that the camp had some women nurses present and the boys were trying to be on their good behavior. An occasional slip would make everybody howl with mirth.

After dinner, the biggest surprise of the evening came in. Monaghan himself carried it with pride. It was a big, four-layer chocolate cake. I hadn't seen such a sight for ages. The boys had all chipped in their ration of chocolate bars to make that cake. On top of the chocolate icing there was a legend in white. It said: THE 449th WELCOMES BACK ITS TOM HARMON OF MICHIGAN! On the side of the cake were two zeros, with a large red "x" of icing crossing out each one. I cut this masterpiece with great care, and everyone stuffed himself happily on it, for this was the treat of treats.

After dinner I had to make a speech, and I gave the squadron a full resume of the fight from where I saw it and of my trip back to the base. As I came to the end of my talk that night, I felt a real lump in my throat. I had been to hundreds of banquets in my life, but never to one like this. I remembered, it seemed like in another world, having made speeches to young boys who lived and slept thinking about football. This occasion was different.

The conclusion of my speech that evening came straight from my heart. I said: "I have had the good fortune to have lunch with the President of the United States. I have enjoyed meeting many of the celebrities of the world, and I once gained a small reputation for playing football for a great team and scoring a few touchdowns. Tonight as I stand here and speak to you, I am not so proud of having had lunch with the President of the United States, although that was a great privilege. I'm not proud of a football record or any name I was lucky enough to make in sports before the war. But I am damned proud that I have been granted the good fortune to be associated with men like you, and I will always be proud that at one time in my life I was a small part of the 449th Fighter Squadron. God bless every one of you." I had never spoken like that before in my life nor said anything I meant one half so sincerely. Those words came right from the core of a plain and simple Irishman. I stood there a moment with tears in my eyes, tears of respect and deep affection for the finest men I have ever known.

THE CHINESE PEOPLE AND THEIR SPIRIT

14

"WHAT DO YOU THINK of the Chinese people?" That is one of the most frequent questions that I have been asked since coming back from China. It would take a whole book to answer that question fully, and it would take a man of greater knowledge than myself to give the real picture of what the Chinese people are. I only know that I like and respect them thoroughly, and that I owe my life to them. If you were to ask any man who has been through the experience of being forced down in Jap-held Chinese territory and helped along by the loyal and valiant Chinese, he would say the same thing. It is impossible to work with the Chinese for any length of time and get to know them without admiring the hard work they do and their great spirit.

The Chinese people seem to have a very simple philosophy of life. They are poor people, or at least most of them are, and they are realistic. They know nothing of the wonderful comforts that Americans take for granted in their homes every day. And yet, the Chinese do not wish to change their way of life. They are one of the hardest working peoples in the world, and they do not need our modern gadgets, or our modern way of living, to be happy. American soldiers in China are apt to compare the country with the United States in external matters, and that is a mistake. The two countries are so different that they cannot be compared on that basis.

In years, our country is the youngest nation on earth, while China has an ancestry that runs back thousands of years. Their history makes ours seem small by comparison. As far as the mechanical side of civilization goes, we are hundreds of years ahead of them in spite of our comparative youth, but for culture and wisdom I am not so sure. They have been satisfied with their ancient way of life and they complain to no one. They seem to have a deep reserve of strength, and though they might on first glance seem backward to an American, pretty soon he begins to wonder. They have got something, all right.

The Chinese know how to work. You can see right away that they do their work with their hearts and souls in it. They don't say much, but their work follows the same lines as that of a bunch of bees or of ants. They work silently and effectively, and although the job may take a little more time, it gets done and done well. They use man power instead of machine power, and they do jobs that no American would even imagine could be done with only bare hands and the most primitive tools.

One afternoon I was in a Chinese tea house. I happened to get to listening to the conversation of the group next to us, and although, of course, I couldn't understand the language, the sound of their voices seemed to express a lot of feeling. An elderly Chinese was doing most of the talking, and I noticed that he kept repeating one word, time and again. There was in the sound of it a kind of animosity that I thought was quite unusual. I asked one of our Chinese interpreters from the field, who happened to be along, what that word meant. He replied, "That word means 'kill' in Chinese, and the old man is talking about the Japanese."

One evening I was in one of the larger towns of China with a few of the other boys. We had happened to be in the neighborhood, and had gone into town with the express purpose of getting a steak and seeing a show. There was one particular restaurant that catered to the Americans in this town, and there you could get a good meal for about four hundred dollars. Chinese dollars, though. In American money that would be about five dollars, but anyway, after five or six months without getting into any town the cost meant very little. A look at the menu of this restaurant would give anybody a laugh if it didn't give him heart failure. Ice cream sold for fifty dollars a dish, and everything else was priced accordingly. The cost may have looked a bit high, but the boys all looked forward to the time when they could get to this town to have some of that fifty dollar ice cream to wind up a steak dinner.

After that evening in town, we went back to base on a shuttle bus run especially for the army. When we got on, there were two Chinese civilians and a Chinese soldier on the bus. The Chinese soldier worked on the airfield and knew that the bus would take the two other Chinese past their homes. When they saw the Chinese on the bus, a couple of enlisted men and one officer began to get sort of tough. They wanted to kick the Chinese off the bus. It was bad enough, I thought, to want to kick the civilians off, but the soldier had been wounded in the foot and it was still bandaged, so that he could not possibly walk back those eight miles to the base. I got mad. There were only two pilots on that bus, but we stuck together. I sounded off with the remark, "It may be okay for you guys to gripe and throw the poor Chinese out of the bus, but there is one thing you guys forget. This is their country, and if you ever get lost out in those hills you may need the Chinese to help you get back, and that soldier may be out there helping you. I say they should ride on this bus if they want to." So the Chinese rode. The soldier thanked me politely when I got out. Some time later I did find out that the Chinese are not only ready but eager to make all kinds of sacrifices and run all kinds of danger to help an American soldier out of a tight spot.

The Chinese seem to exist okay on a diet that a normal American would starve on. They eat rice three hundred and sixty days out of the year, at least. I have seen five coolies eat a full bucket of rice at one sitting. I tried living on their diet of rice and greens for a period of three days once, and when those days were over I never wanted to look at rice again. To make matters worse, the rice or the uncooked greens gave me the worst case of dysentery that I've ever had. You just couldn't get away from rice in China. When I got back home, the first five times I was invited out for dinner they served rice. Each time I looked at my host in amazement, and as I kept being served rice I was convinced it was a joke on me. The fifth dinner I was invited to and confronted with rice, I broke down and asked my host if my friends were kidding me! They weren't, but everybody laughed at my predicament and I didn't have to eat the rice to be polite.

The Chinese have the greatest, most determined spirit I have ever witnessed. Their work to defeat Japan takes the concentrated effort of every Chinese in the world, I am sure. For sheer grit, the Chinese take a back seat to nobody in this world. I have worked with them, and I have seen them grit their teeth and take all the punishment the Japs can deliver. They know that their time will come, and until then they just grin and bear it. They are biding their time until they can really strike back and take their vengeance.

The Chinese workers on our airfield in China were one hundred percent trustworthy, and they could work like twice their weight in manpower. I remembered what a hard time I had had washing down Little Butch II before starting out from Africa as I watched the two Chinese boys doing the same job with soap and water to our various planes as a matter of daily routine. They kept those babies clean as a whistle, and it was quite a job, as there was always a lot of dirt and oil to be washed off. They knew we were there to help them get rid of the Japs, and apparently they felt their elbow grease could not be expended in a greater cause.

The Chinese may know that we consider the Japs as our enemies, but so far as they are concerned, they consider the Japs as their personal enemies and they will do any job they can to help run the Japs out of their country. The Allies have been giving China a little help, but so far it is just a drop in the bucket. China has little chance of beating the Japs soon by herself, for the Japs are well equipped for modern mechanized warfare with tanks, planes, and all sorts of modern weapons. The Chinese have almost nothing, but they fight the Japs with everything they can lay their hands on. They use rocks, clubs, weapons captured from the Japs, anything and everything. I have seen Chinese soldiers carrying guns that I swear must have been left over from our own Civil War. With all their difference in equipment, though, China will never be defeated by Japan. The Japs may torture and plunder China for years, but they cannot win. In the end the Chinese will come out on top, just because of their dogged power to take it.

Chinese marriage is not like ours. They pick their mates for the amount of work they can do and their ability to bear strong children. Apparently the element of love as we understand it plays no part. The value they look for is working ability, and the women as well as the men labor hard and long.

Girls, however, are held of little account. The orphanages in China are mostly tenanted by little Chinese girl children who have been abandoned by their parents. Quite a few of the boys at our base "adopted" little Chinese orphans at the mission in the neighboring town. That meant they would leave a certain amount of money with the good nuns and the "adopted" child's food, clothing and education would be paid for a year or two. It was a strange sight to see those hardy and tough soldiers of the American Air Force come into the mission and watch the little orphans come running at once to their adopted fathers, chattering away gaily. They never mistook which one was their adopted father, and would sit on his lap all afternoon. They were good-natured, cute little things, and the boys liked to do things for them. When Christmas time came, they would take the candy that had been sent to them from home over to the mission for the little girls. The joy in those little faces was worth all the candy in the world. When the squadron invited all the orphans out to the base for a movie and party before Christmas, the soldiers tried hard to act sort of hard-boiled, but these small children melted their hearts down as if they were soft butter. The children enjoyed the party, and their natural politeness and graceful ways were something to watch. We couldn't do much to help the good sisters in their work for the orphans, but we did all we could.

Not all the missions were as lucky as ours. One mission up closer to the front lines suffered torture and ruin because they had helped the Doolittle fliers to escape the Japs. When word reached the mission from runners that the Japs were coming after them, the Bishop who was the head organized an escape. All the nuns, the other priests, and all the children over three years old went up into the mountains. One of the priests stayed behind to look after the tiny children, who could not possibly have traveled and who they thought would be safe from the Japs because they were so young. The refugees from the mission lived in hiding up in the mountains for three weeks, with what little supplies the loyal Chinese could smuggle to them. The Japs at times were no more than half a mile away from them, but they did not discover their hiding place. After three weeks, they returned to their mission. They had received word that the Japs had gone back to their own lines and given up the search. What they found when they returned was too terrible to tell.

Just before I left China, the U.S. forces had been bolstered by the addition of the Chinese American Wing. This group was made up of Chinese airmen who had been trained in the United States. The Chinese pilots have already proved that they can stay in there with the Japs and swap blow for blow any time. The only fault the American pilots find with their Chinese colleagues is that they want to do nothing but kill Japs. That may sound like a silly criticism, but in combat the fighters who go out on raids as bomber protection must stay with the bombers. That is their duty. Chinese pilots, when they see a Zero, seem to lose their heads sometimes in their fierce desire to shoot down that Jap, and they have often left the bombers to shift for themselves while they pursued a stray Zero. Chinese pilots have been operating for some time with the American pilots in China. For them the missions imply a double risk, for if they are shot down and fall into enemy hands their chance of living doesn't amount to a hill of beans. That doesn't matter to them, though, and every flight they can fly is flown.

The hatred of the Chinese toward the Japs is something almost beyond belief. It has been aroused by the atrocities the Japs have committed in China to a white heat that is past anything we Americans can conceive of. I once saw Chinese children walking through a town dragging something on a long string, and that thing they dragged a human arm. As the children moved along with their gruesome toy, the people spat on it. I was astounded and almost sick at the sight. I learned that the object thus dragged in the dirt was part of the body of a Jap pilot who had been shot down the day before and killed in the crash of his plane. I couldn't understand how anybody could have such hatred in his soul until I thought of some of the experiences the Chinese have suffered at the hands of the Japs. Such expression of hatred as this may seem bestial to some of us sheltered Americans, but until we have suffered some of the terrible provocation that the Chinese have suffered we have no right to judge. We don't realize what the hardships of war are in a ravaged country.

I think it would be a good thing if the folks at home got mad enough to feel a little of that hatred which the Chinese have for their enemy. When I returned to the States, I spoke to a few groups of people in Detroit. One of the things I said was that maybe a good bombing would do us Americans good. Immediately I began receiving letters of protest against this statement. They were mostly anonymous letters, and the terms they used were pretty abusive. I didn't think

Chinese coolies inspect ruins of Jap Zero motor. The Chinese always look for Jap pilots or air crew members.

much of those letters. If those letter writers had gone through half of what our allies the Chinese have suffered, they would know what I mean.

I think the Chinese are one of the finest peoples in the whole world. I respect and admire their spirit and the way they have risen to the demands of this dread time in human history. As for what they have done for me on more than one occasion, I can never thank them enough.

ONE PILOT'S PRAYER

15

I STAYED AT THE base for about two weeks after the memorable night of my return. I wanted to stay with the squadron and gain back my strength there, but the Doc thought otherwise. He sent me to the Base Hospital at the headquarters of the 14th Air Force. There I was given a complete physical checkup. They said my burns were healing in fine shape, although it would be some time before the scars left my legs. I thought I didn't mind a few scars, now I was back with the boys and had escaped imprisonment or worse from the Japs.

After about ten days in the hospital I was allowed to return to the squadron. The boys had been flying missions right along and doing fine against the Japs. They were beginning to have a very impressive record. So far they had averaged eleven Jap planes for every one that we had lost. But that record, good as it looked, also told the story of the boys who had lost their lives in those fights. It made you stop and think.

One day I was called to the Commanding Officer's office and told that my orders for returning to the United States had gone into headquarters. I was to be sent home! When I heard that news, I got sort of choked up with emotion. Home! The word alone was enough to bring a lump in the throat. I was really going back to see Mom and Dad, the whole family, and Butch. It was a wonderful sensation.

My next sensation, a little while afterwards, was one of sadness. I hated the thought of leaving the squadron and the boys. After all, I had learned to live this kind of life and to think of home as a very far away place. If I were to go, I wished I could take all the boys back with me. The last few days I was with the squadron, they all kidded around a lot about my going home, but I could see how much they all wished that they were going too.

I had decided I would surprise Mom, so I didn't write to let her know I was coming. I thought I would just walk in on her some day and take a good look at her face. It would be a sight worth seeing. I decided to let Elyse know in advance, so I wrote her a happy letter all full of the good word. I was looking forward to the trip home, but most of all to the day I got back to Ann Arbor.

I received a wire from headquarters that my orders were waiting for me and that I was to report at 14th Air Force Headquarters at once. The next day I left our base. I was sorry to go, and those last handshakes with some of the boys just about killed me, but at the same time my mind was already set on what was ahead and leaving wasn't quite as bad as I thought it would be. It was not until much later that I was to miss the 449th fully. For the moment, I was anxious to get going on the homeward route.

The weather was a little bad the day I left, and only one transport came in. I climbed aboard. This transport was due to hit the other front line bases before going back to headquarters and so I went along for a little ride. We stopped at one base, then went on to another. Mac, our pilot, who had had plenty of experience hauling the big defenseless DC-3 transport around the front line bases, decided he would leave the passengers at this base and pick us up on his way back. His decision turned out to be a lucky one as well as wise. After he had unloaded his cargo, he lost an engine and had to return to our base on only one. He was skipping over the mountains when the engine cut out on him, and it was just as well he didn't have any load either of cargo or passengers. He did a beautiful job and got the big transport in safely, but the engine had to be changed. This meant a layover at one of the hottest bases in China. The next morning, while we were waiting for a new engine to be flown in, the Japs came in on a strafing attack. Everyone was in the bomb shelters, and I was standing in the doorway watching the little green devils cut the grounded ships to ribbons. The P-40's and the newer P-51's were in the air and had jumped the top-cover Zeros. They knocked down eight of them without a single loss to our forces. But there were just not enough of our ships in the air to catch the top cover and the strafing Zeros both. As I stood in that doorway, a Zero swooped to closer than five hundred feet above us. Then there were two more. It seemed to me that I had never seen three Zeros go that slowly. I had a tremendous desire to have Little Butch II and come zooming in on them with a little parting present made of lead.

The Japs finished their job and went home. This was my last look at the Japs and their Zero. I thought again that the Zero sure is a good looking plane to watch, and it's too bad it has to be flown by a bunch of madmen who think they can run the world.

Late that afternoon another transport came in. The first one had been cut to shreds by the Jap bullets that strafed the field that morning, so the new engine that was brought in for her was useless. We all piled into the second transport and I started again on the first lap of the trip home.

I checked in for my orders at Group Headquarters that night. They were not due for a day or so, and I had two days of rest at the base. Schultz had come back to headquarters to have some wisdom teeth taken care of by the only dentist we had in China. Together Bob and I saw the town and had some steaks. While we were making the rounds one night, one of the boys came in with the news that Schultz had been made Captain. That was news that really called for a celebration. We talked long and late that night over a bottle of "jing-bao" juice. I was happy that Schultz had got his captaincy, for he certainly deserved it. It seemed sort of sad that after all we had gone through together we were going to be separated now. I hated to think of leaving the old war horse. I knew I would miss his razzing. I wished he could come home with me, because Schultz had been flying more than anybody else in the squadron and I thought it was beginning to show on him. He needed a rest just as much as I did.

We made a million plans that night. We planned how we would get together at the football games in Ann Arbor after the war. We thought of all the good times we would have together in the years to come. Later on I said a silent prayer that the Big Boss upstairs would see fit to grant us those favors. Captain Bob Schultz looked like a beaten dog that night. He wanted to go home so bad that he could taste it.

The following morning we went to the line to see about getting transportation back to India over the Hump. When I showed my orders in the office the boys all just gazed, and felt the paper. The sight of those orders to go home was for them practically a glimpse at heaven. The look in their eyes really hit me.

I arranged to catch a China National Airways ship over the Hump.

Because the Japs were always fooling around with those cargo planes, the pilot knew all the tricks. He had been with the Flying Tigers and he was really good.

A few hours before I left I had had a short talk with General Chennault. I was asked to report in his office, and did so immediately. I saluted and came to attention as I reported, but the General put me at ease at once. He asked me to carry some documents to India for him and some others all the way to the States. I was glad I had the opportunity to speak with him before leaving the China theater, because to me General Chennault is *the* General. I will never forget my two brief meetings with him.

Schultz went to the plane with me. We said goodbye. We had both dreaded this moment, but we managed to bring it off as casually as if we were to see each other next week back at the base.

The big transport took off, and we had a good ride to India. From the base across the Hump, I caught a B-25 going back to Delhi. The ride was long, but welcome. In Delhi I waited three days for another transport, then went on to Karachi.

I knew that Bill Bolton was somewhere in Karachi. Bill had been flying so much that he became exhausted and had to be sent home for a rest about a month before. When he had got out of the transport at Karachi, he had a sudden attack of paralysis. He was placed in an iron lung, and everybody hoped for the best. It was a sad moment for the boys when they heard about Bill. He had been a perfect flight leader and was one of the best liked boys in the squadron. I spent what time I had in Karachi trying to find out if Bill was there but I was unable to find him.

Because I was a courier for the General, I was able to board one of the Army's greatest transports for Dakar. It was a long flight over rough land with plenty of updrafts and so on. On the plane were some wounded men who didn't fare too well so far as air sickness was concerned. I felt, though, that we were lucky to get a transport going that whole lap of the journey.

At Dakar, I found I was still "sweating it out" about flying the ocean. However, we took off and the rest of the trip home was uneventful. We crossed the great expanse of ocean, and we went over the South American jungles. We stopped at Trinidad, and from there went on toward Puerto Rico. About an hour out of Puerto Rico, over the ocean, the pilot almost lost one of his engines. My heart did a double beat. With the load of passengers we had on that plane, we

Lieutenant Tom Harmon and Miss Elyse "Butch" Knox, after whom Little Butch I and II were named.

Tom with Dad and Mom Harmon.

could never have stayed in the air if that engine had gone out. But then it caught again. We landed at Puerto Rico and had a brief lunch there. When the plane soared up into the sky again it flew like a homing bird. It was the final hop, and there was a tremendous eagerness in the hearts of all the boys on the plane. You felt it in the atmosphere.

At about nine o'clock that evening the sky ahead seemed to light up. It was Miami in the distance. The faces of every person in the plane hit a higher glow than the light in the sky. What a sight that was! The lights of home.

Before long the big ship hit the runway and we were down. Back to God's country. I climbed out of that plane and stooped to kiss the ground. I felt wonderful.

We went through customs and then were assigned rooms in the barracks. I could hardly restrain myself from telephoning Mom and Dad, but I had made up my mind to surprise them and that was what I intended to do.

That night as I lay in my bunk I could hardly sleep for all the excitement that was filling me. I remembered the feeling I had had when I left the United States. That night I had said a special prayer. I asked the Lord above to watch over me and help me so that some day I could get back to our beloved country and my folks safe and sound I remembered that prayer, and now I said another very special one. I asked the Lord to watch over the rest of the boys and give comfort to those families whose sons would not return. I gave thanks for all I had received, for my wonderful family and for the true friends I had, friends who would stick to a man through thick and thin. I asked the Big Boss to help me to be worthy of all these.

I was home! I was no hero, and I didn't want to be, but it was a satisfaction to have been in there socking. I hoped a couple of my socks had done a little good.

I lay in my cot, and my mind flashed across the hundreds of miles of American earth to Mom and Dad and the family, then in thought I leaped the Rockies to Butch, and then I thought of home again. I was in the United States! I began to drift off to sleep, and a saying of General MacArthur's crossed my mind. THERE ARE NO ATHEISTS IN FOXHOLES. Truer words were never spoken, but the thought of that truth in relation to the Air Force Boys came into my mind. I wanted to add to that statement, PILOTS ALSO PRAY. I knew that first hand, and my prayers had been heard. I was home!

END